SILENSOPHY

First Edition

By

Subhash Vasist

Silensophy

First Edition, April 2025

ISBN 978-93-341-2978-6

Subjects: Philosophy, Psychology, Meditation

MRP ₹399

Distribution:
Powered by Pothi.com

DEDICATION

My deepest gratitude to all the teachers
who have happened to me in this journey of self-discovery.

PREFACE

As all the raindrops fallen from the sky, flows into the ocean, so are we with life's progression. We all are in movement, in search for something. We explore the world, embark on dreams, chase goals and often we find ourselves caught in the web of life. We experience the pull and push between our past choices and future aspirations. We are on a rollercoaster ride on the waves of emotions, of success and failures. There comes a point in all our lives when our search culminates. We embark ourselves in search of true happiness, peace and meaning of life.

In this book I share with you a simple and practical way to self-discovery and inner transformation. I hold with certainty that Stillness is the easiest way to reconnect with your true self. It is the foundation of clarity, peace, and wisdom. The more you function from this center of Stillness, the more you will uncover the peace and wisdom that resides within you. Where ever you are in your journey of life, this book is here to guide you and set you on the right course towards truth and realization.

I invite you to embark on this adventure of self-realization, that unfolds with every breath and every moment. May the wisdom serve you as a beacon of light, and may you find within yourself the infinite reservoir of peace, love, and wisdom that has always been there, waiting to be awakened.

With love,
Subhash Vasist

SILENSOPHY

Silence is often viewed as an inconvenience, a void, something that must be filled – with more information, more entertainment, more noise. The distractions of modern life – technology, social media, endless obligations – pull us in multiple directions. Our mind is constantly being drawn towards perceived sources of happiness – success, material wealth, external validation. In this pursuit, we often lose touch with our inner selves – our center. As we move farther away from our center, we feel more restless, anxious, and disconnected. To overcome these states of unrest, we seek gratifications in fleeting pleasures or external achievements, but they are only temporary. Lasting peace, clarity, and fulfillment can only be found when we are centered – by cultivating Stillness.

Silence is not merely the absence of sound. Silence is not emptiness but fullness; not absence, but presence. It is a dynamic, living force that allows us to see beyond the surface of things. When we silence the noise and constant chatter of the mind, we begin to experience our Self. It is in these moments of deep Stillness that we confront our deepest fears, desires, and questions. We meet ourselves as we truly are, without the layers of external conditioning. Silence serves as a gateway to self-discovery and realization.

In this quiet space, we begin to understand that we are more than the roles we play or the labels we carry. Not defined by our careers, achievements, or possessions, we become receptive to the subtler dimensions of existence. Through the practice of Stillness, we can reconnect with this deeper sense of Self, and from this place of grounded awareness, we can live life with greater authenticity, purpose, and peace.

The practice of Stillness is integrated deep within spiritual practices of all traditions and faith. Everyone can practice Stillness without having to move away from your roots of tradition and culture. You will realize that this practice of Stillness is an enabler to explore your own roots and traditions in a much better way while also enabling you to recognize the oneness in all forms of spiritual practices. While different traditions employ various methods to cultivate stillness – breath control, chanting, music, visualization, yoga – the core philosophy or the essence transcends technique. Stillness, ultimately, is the state of pure awareness, unconditioned by thoughts, emotions, or sensory distractions.

Stillness is not to be understood as inactivity but a profound receptivity which allows one to perceive reality as it is, beyond the distortions of restless thought.

Life's deepest meaning is found not in what we achieve, but in how we experience and engage with the world. Whether we are experiencing success or failure, joy or sorrow, the practice of Stillness allows us to remain anchored in the present. When we are rooted in Stillness, we engage with the world from a place of clarity and wisdom. We become less reactive, less driven by fear or desire, and more aligned with our true nature. It is an invitation to slow down, to listen deeply, and to reconnect with the Stillness that lies at the heart of existence. It is a way of living.

What is Stillness and how do we develop it?

A laboratory is a place where we conduct experiments. We often conduct experiments to observe and analyze outcomes. An experiment can result in the desired outcome or the experiment can fail. If the experiment fails, we do another trial or conduct a new experiment. The most important activity in an experiment is observation. Practicing Stillness is akin to entering a laboratory where the aim is simply to observe. By sitting still, you give the mind a chance to rest, which marks the beginning of a journey into the Self. In the laboratory of our Self, we are to observe all that has happened and that which is happening.

Consider a simple experiment. Take a clear glass container and fill it with water. The water turns cloudy when you add a little mud into it. In order to restore clarity, we need to simply wait and allow the mud to settle. Any effort to stir or interfere only disrupts the mud from settling. In life, there are times when doing nothing is essential. Practicing Stillness is like witnessing the settling of mud in the container, and the awareness we encounter is like the resulting clarity of the water as the mud settles.

When we entered this world, we were like that clear water. The mud represents the conditioning, experiences, and challenges that life has presented to us thus far. While we cannot avoid these life situations, they tend to obscure our original clarity. Practice of Stillness is the process of returning to that clear, undisturbed state.

As for the glass of muddy water which is something external, you could simply leave it alone to clear by itself. But such is not the case with our Self. The container, water, and mud all represents an aspect of the Self. Only 'you' can watch the mud settle within your Self. Without this attentive witnessing, inner disturbances will persist, disrupting clarity. Observing oneself is fundamental to the practice of Stillness.

In Stillness, you may focus your attention, perhaps on your breath, which requires effort and mental focus. This is called 'concentration.' When you analyze or ponder a topic, this is 'contemplation.' When you examine your own mind, thoughts, feelings and motivation, we call this 'Introspection'. All these activities involve the mind, requiring mental effort and, thus, is not true Stillness. Yet, they are valuable exercises in understanding the constructs of the Self.

What, then, about silence? If 'silence' means 'silencing the mind,' this still needs efforts. True Stillness is not about controlling or engaging the mind but simply observing. Imagine the mind as a stirrer in your glass container: any movement will disturb the settling mud. Instead of stirring, you watch without acting. Who, then, is the observer if it is not your mind?

The practice of Stillness is the discipline of entering the laboratory of the Self. By observing the mind, emotions, and everything occurring within and around you, you move deeper in to your Self. As your practice deepens, you move beyond the constructs of the mind and even the Self.

Celebrate life

Live every moment joyfully

Contents

BEGINNING

Chapter One

Journey of a seed

"The best time to plant a tree was twenty years ago,
And the next best time is now."

From the very first breath, our perceptions and understanding are molded by the world around us. Before we embark on the inward journey to the Self, let us explore the journey of a plant seed. Seeds come in many shapes and sizes, each holding a mystery of potential. One never knows what a tiny seed can become until it is planted and grows. It is astonishing how a plant or tree is hidden within a small seed. For instance, the seed of a cedar tree is only a few millimeters in size, yet a full-grown cedar can reach heights of about two hundred feet.

A seed is the beginning of a plant's journey. It is packed with nutrition and instructions – the genetic information – needed to become a large plant. The seed's journey into becoming a plant is transformational. Interestingly, a seed never sees its own sprouting. It must completely transform itself to become a sprout. There is no other way.

The Earth serves as a kind of springboard. A seed is planted, and a plant emerges. Without the right conditions, a seed remains dormant, as though asleep. The right conditions enable transformation. In nature, we observe that a seed rarely sprouts in daylight. The necessary elements for growth and nutrition are hidden in the darkness of the earth. Once sown in the soil, the seed stretches itself from the inside and springs toward the sun. Darkness seems to be a necessary ingredient for growth and transformation. A seed journeys from darkness and emerges as a sprout into the light.

> The Journey of a seed gives us insight on the movement of gross matter into subtleness.

A seed's transformation into a sprout symbolizes courage in the face of the unknown. It takes courage for the seed to let go of being a seed. In letting go, it transforms into a sprout. Without this courage, the seed would remain a seed and eventually perish.

Have you ever wondered, what is the goal of the seed? Why does it struggle to transform? What is it searching for? A seed is in continuous movement – from a seed to a sprout, to a sapling, to a young plant, and finally to a full-grown plant or tree. As the plant grows, it unfurls its branches like open arms and dresses itself in a tapestry of green leaves. There is an exchange – of nutrients, sunlight, water, and air. Flowers bloom in all their colors, dancing in the air, romancing the sun, as if flowering is the seed's expression of why it transformed. The blooming of the flower gives meaning to the seed's journey. These flowers offer their fragrance, the essence of the seed. The cycle of birth continues as flowers turn into fruits and new seeds are formed.

The journey of a seed offers insight into the movement from gross matter to subtleness. At each stage, the plant ascends into greater subtlety – from the roots, to the stem, to the branches, to the delicate leaves, and finally to the flower. Flowers are the most delicate. The peak of subtleness is in the fragrance, where the seed disappears into the vast sky. Through its fragrance, the seed transcends itself into eternity, finding its way to freedom.

In this journey, we see how the gross matter – the earth – becomes one with the subtle – the sky. Bridging the earth and the sky is the life of the plant.

You might ask, what about the fruits and seeds that follow the flower? The journey into fruits and seeds is the return of subtleness back into the gross form of nature. This is life completing its cycle.

Ordinarily, we draw boundaries between the earth, the plant, and the sky. But at a macro level, they are part of a single continuum.

Observing the journey of a seed can unravel many aspects of the human psyche and our connection to the universe.

Chapter Two

Crisis at hand

"The journey to self-discovery begins in silence."

Chuang Tzu was sitting in a contemplative mood. A friend came looking for him. He asked Chaung Tzu, "what are you dreaming about?" and Chaung Tzu started to share his dream. He said "I was thinking about the meaning of life while sitting by the Cedar tree. I gradually felt sleepy and I went to sleep. In my dream, I was flying up above the fields. I looked around and saw that I had wings, large and beautiful. I was flapping them. I had turned into a butterfly! It was a great feeling of joy. I was experiencing freedom. I felt light and carefree. I was flying around any way I wished. The dream felt absolutely real. I had forgotten that I was Chuang Tzu. I was simply a butterfly".

His friend said, "sounds like a wonderful dream". Chuang Tzu said, "for a moment I had forgotten I was

Chaung Tzu. When I woke up, I realized that I was Chuang Tzu. This puzzles me."

His friend said, "What is puzzling about it? Dream is a dream, why take it so seriously?"

Chaung Tzu said, "What if I am dreaming right now? Everything right now feels real, same as the dream I had. What if I am not Chaung Tzu, but the butterfly who is dreaming of being Chuang Tzu?"

His friend said, "Well, Let me pinch you, so you can feel my pinch, so you know that this is real and that was a dream." Chuang Tzu said, "What if you are part of the dream that the butterfly is having?"

This is an existential question. But much before this, why was Chaung Tzu dreaming of a butterfly?

We are all looking for freedom. A child, as soon as it learns to crawl, feels excited to crawl fast. When a child learns to stand on two legs, they run around for no reason at all. As the child learns to ride a bicycle, they want to go really fast. In adolescence, young boys want to go fast on their bikes. Speeding seems to be a natural instinct. It is an expression of pursuing freedom – the taste of independence. Chuang Tzu's dream of flying high in the air is a similar expression. Deep down, he has a desire for freedom. Even as adults, we are in a race, chasing our passion and careers. Hidden beneath all this is our innate desire to set ourselves free.

As living beings, we all have limits when it comes to physical growth. While our physical development reaches a certain point, the mind possesses the capacity for continual expansion. It is continuously looking to expand its horizons. This expansion is made visible through the accumulation of power, prestige, property, materialistic wealth, etc. Expansionism can be seen in societies, communities, organizations, and even nations.

The heights you wish to achieve in life depends on your investment in a solid foundation. A cedar tree must invest in its roots to grow tall. The deeper the roots, the taller the tree. Roots are its foundation. Soil plays an important role in the growth of a cedar. Soil can be understood as the necessary conditioning – the environment.

There is an art form to grow miniaturized trees called Bonsai. Creating a bonsai involves carefully cultivating a young tree through a combination of pruning, wiring, and potting techniques to mimic the appearance of a mature, full-sized tree in miniature. The plant is regularly pruned to shape its branches and control growth, while wiring is used to shape the branches into the desired form. The taproot is cut, and the roots are pruned and contained within a shallow pot, limiting the tree's growth and contributing to its miniature size. Plant roots are very sensitive, they can sense the soil. By cutting the taproot and settling in shallow, loose soil, the plant confines its growth, unable to realize its full potential.

> To understand your potential, you need to understand your conditionings.

If you make a bonsai out of a cedar, the tree cannot reach its true potential. The tree has potential, but it cannot grow. Depth in the roots is necessary to propel growth. Much damage is done to the cedar tree. The tree has lost its true identity. Man seems to decide how tall a cedar should grow and how its shape should be. He wants to be in total control. This desire to control can be seen in his interactions with the environment, relationships, and even in other life endeavors. While man's desire to control and shape his environment has led to great achievements, it sometimes distances him from the natural world.

To understand your potential, you need to understand the soil – your conditioning. To develop your roots, you need to prepare the soil to establish a firm ground – your understanding, your foundation. Only when you establish a strong foundation can your roots find depth.

It is important to recognize the role of parents, teachers, society, and their influence and impact on to the soil you are on. The quality of soil is an indicator of your growth potential. As a child, you depend on your parents, teachers, and society for your development, but there comes a time when you have to become responsible for the soil you are rooted in. What has been your own role in preparing the soil?

Recognizing our own life conditioning can give insights into why we are the way we are. It requires discipline to further prepare the soil. You take charge of cultivating the soil necessary for your future growth.

Ordinarily, we are unaware of our conditioning. Conditioning over time turns into familiarity. Familiarity gives us a sense of safety – our comfort zone. Given a choice we always chose to be in our comfort zone. Even if we are in an uncomfortable situation, we may opt to stay in it only because we are familiar with it. The longer we are in our comfort zone, the harder it is to change. This is the same with our conditioning. The longer we stay conditioned, the deeper it affects our being. Growth cannot happen when one is comfortable. Being uncomfortable is a necessary ingredient for growth. A seed has to come out of its shell in order to sprout and grow. Awareness is necessary to recognize our conditionings. It is necessary to reflect on why we are the way we are. What conditioning has shaped us? Courage and a strong spirit is necessary to overcome conditioning and further shape our growth.

For example, observe the quality of life we lead. We may often find that it has declined significantly as compared to what our previous generations may have experienced. This decline has been unfolding across generations. Each successive generation experiencing a further decline in quality of life. You might argue that, with advances in science, technology, and more comfortable lifestyles, humanity is better off than it was decades ago. It is worthwhile to go deeper on aspects that have affected our quality of life.

> The practice of Stillness gives you the opportunity to establish a strong foundation for yourself.

Health comes at a price. The food we eat is not natural or organic anymore. The salt we consume has lost its original richness. The alarming levels of pesticides in our food is just one example of how disconnected we have become from nature. We are more comfortable popping pills than eating healthy.

Human relationship is on a decline – another consequence of our own making. We may have countless acquaintances on social media, but lack real friendships. Technology is replacing genuine communication. Today we are more comfortable talking to a robot than to people. Stress levels have reached unprecedented heights, and the constant distractions of modern life have shortened our attention spans to mere seconds. This in itself, is a crisis.

If life were truly progressive, each generation would have become richer – not only in wealth but in wisdom, kindness, happiness, and peace. It is important to reflect on what are we actually handing over from our generation to the next.

Centuries have passed since the first civilization, and one might think humanity would have moved beyond mere survival. Yet, reality shows otherwise. With each passing generation, wisdom is receding, and we are losing our roots. Today many from the farming community have moved to the cities for better lifestyle. Many farmers no longer know how to cultivate crops in the traditional way, and communities have forgotten the local knowledge of herbs. What was once common sense now needs schooling, as the wisdom is no longer available. Increasingly, knowledge is imported from outside, and we are left without a legacy to carry forward – a crisis in motion.

Many people seem comfortable in their own bubbles, ignoring the imbalance created in the name of advancement. Indigenous wisdom reminds us, '*When the last tree is cut down, the last fish eaten, and the last stream poisoned, you will realize that you cannot eat money.*' Restoring balance in this world seems to be a monumental task, one that requires a unified effort from an entire generation. But before we scale the problem to the entire world and look at solving the problems of the world, it becomes important to look at oneself and start with the Self. The Self is a whole world in itself. It is important to question and be conscious of what foot prints are we contributing to as we journey through this world.

Chapter Three

Great divide

"In Stillness we see things as they are"

There is a local saying: '*weigh your words before you speak.*' Often, words have been overused or misused, which has led to drifting of words far from their original meanings. What once held a deeper significance has, over time, taken on a more casual tone.

Language is not merely a tool for communication; it is a vessel through which cultures have conveyed their deepest values, beliefs, and practices. When the meanings of words evolve or are diluted, the underlying philosophies they represent often erode. This semantic shift has impacted us on how we think, communicate, and experience culture.

Traditional practices such as meditation, spirituality, rituals, and ethical frameworks have been transmitted through words and symbols, both of which are deeply embedded within our culture's linguistic heritage. As our societies modernize, practices that once held sacred or philosophical value are often repackaged to fit contemporary, commodified frameworks.

Take, for instance, the concept of yoga. What was once regarded as an integrative practice aimed at spiritual liberation (moksha) and self-realization (atma-jnana) has increasingly been reduced, in popular discourse, to a mere fitness routine emphasizing physical flexibility and relaxation. The semantic shift here is not benign; it actively narrows the philosophical depth of yoga, divorcing it from its metaphysical roots.

Meditation, likewise, has suffered from a similar transformation. Traditionally, meditation was intended as a disciplined method of transcending the mind's limitations, achieving heightened states of awareness, and ultimately realizing one's unity with the greater reality. However, in contemporary usage, the term has often been diluted to signify relaxation techniques aimed solely at stress reduction – an important benefit, but a shallow interpretation of a profound spiritual discipline. In daily life, we find it easier to watch a movie than to meditate. We find it difficult to disengage from the daily barrage of distractions.

This semantic shift is not merely linguistic; it reflects and accelerates a broader cultural decline. As terms are redefined to fit modern, often materialistic paradigms, the values associated with them fade into the background. Instead, convenience, productivity, and superficial wellness take their place.

This decline in values is self-reinforcing. As we grow up exposed only to the diluted meanings of these practices, the deeper wisdom they once conveyed becomes increasingly inaccessible. The traditional frameworks that upheld societal ethics, spiritual growth, and individual fulfillment have become reduced to cultural relics that are acknowledged but not genuinely understood or practiced. We are often in a state of confusion; lost in what is right and what is wrong. Entangled in worldly pursuits, we are drawn further away from the experience of meeting ourselves. We know much about the outside world, yet very little about our own being. This is the 'great divide'.

The danger of this process is subtle but pervasive. When words lose their connection to their original, expansive meanings, the values they represent also diminish. A culture that forgets its roots becomes susceptible to fragmentation, losing both its cohesion and its capacity for meaningful progress.

A conscious effort must be made to preserve not just the external forms of traditional practices, but their underlying philosophical foundations. This involves a reclamation of language, ensuring that terms related to spirituality, meditation, and ethical living are used in ways that honor their intended depth and significance.

ESTABLISHING ROOTS

Chapter Four

Science and Art

"Science and art,
Both require, keen observation."

The mind is constantly learning, continuously processing and evaluating information from the environment through our senses. It is continuously assessing unfamiliar inputs. Any new stimuli naturally heighten our attention, triggering the brain's alertness to new inputs. However, when encountering familiar or repetitive information, the mind's response diminishes. To optimize efficiency, the brain forms patterns and mental shortcuts, a process known as *schema formation*. This evolutionary adaptation allows the mind to conserve cognitive resources, enabling quicker and more efficient processing of familiar experiences while reserving alertness for new or unexpected stimuli. Imagine life, if you had to process all the letters A-Z the same way as you had processed it when you first learnt to read and write? Life would become very complicated if you had to process everything each time.

When something is very familiar, we may assume that we already understand it without taking the time to analyze it thoroughly. This can lead to overlooking nuances or important details. When something is very familiar it has the potential to be overlooked. However, this does not mean that the mind completely ignores known information. It is more about allocating attention and cognitive resources efficiently. Known information is stored in memory and is quickly retrieved when required. It does not need the same level of conscious attention as when something new or unexpected is encountered. This is applicable to words, ideas, thoughts and emotions.

> Unlearning is like taking a step back from something you know really well.

Our perceptions play a crucial role in shaping our reality. Perceptions are the way we interpret and make sense of information from our physical senses, experiences, and beliefs. Over a period of time, perceptions can grow stronger and become our reality that we live in. They can significantly influence how we experience and interpret the world around us. When these perceptions become particularly strong, they can color our overall understanding of reality. This process is influenced by various factors, including emotions, personal experiences, cultural background, and cognitive biases.

A cognitive bias is a systematic pattern of deviation from rationality in judgment, whereby individuals create their own subjective reality based on their perception, experiences, and mental shortcuts. These biases can cause people to make irrational or inconsistent decisions, often as a result of cognitive shortcuts the brain uses to process complex information quickly. Common examples include 1) favoring information that confirms one's existing beliefs; 2) relying on immediate examples that come to mind; 3) being heavily influenced by the first piece of information encountered. While cognitive biases help us navigate the world efficiently, they can also lead to errors in reasoning, flawed decision-making, and distorted perspectives.

It is important to recognize the power of perception and its impact on our thoughts, emotions, and behaviors. Being aware of our perceptions and understanding that they are not always an absolute reflection of reality can contribute to a more adaptive mindset – what we call as 'openness'. With openness, unlearning becomes a possibility.

Imagine you are looking out of a window. If you get really close, the window might start to disappear because it is so close to your eyes. You might forget that it is even there! But if you step back, the window becomes clear again, and you are able to recognize it.

Unlearning is like taking a step back from something you know really well, as in the case of stepping away from the window to see it clearly. It helps you notice and remember things you might have forgotten because they were too close. So, unlearning is like giving your brain a chance to see familiar things in a new way.

When you hear, 'Pain is like a door that helps you pay attention,' you might pause and consider its meaning. We often pay little attention to our bodies – that is, until something hurts. When we feel discomfort, like a sore knee or a fever, it demands our attention, drawing us to understand our physical state more closely. In this way, pain, though unpleasant, becomes a tool that heightens our awareness of our physical Self.

Language is a powerful tool for learning, yet once we have acquired knowledge, that very learning can sometimes obstruct our ability to grasp new insights. So, how do we unlearn?

Consider the statement, 'A person could see through his ears.' Instinctively, your mind might react, "Wait, that's not right! Eyes are for seeing, not ears." But what if I were to say, "Ears have eyes?" This invites us to explore alternative ways of thinking about our understanding.

A person with eyesight perceives the world through their eyes. In contrast, someone who cannot see, engages all their senses and their entire body to comprehend their surroundings. This perspective can deepen our understanding, revealing that the very things we think we know can become barriers to embracing new ideas.

Imagine a vast dictionary within your brain, filled with words you have learnt throughout your life. Each word is mapped to meanings and contexts, intertwined with emotions shaped by your experiences. When you hear or use specific words, they evoke feelings such as joy, sadness, excitement, and more. To truly grasp new meanings of words you believe you already understand, you may need to tread carefully, allowing yourself the opportunity to experience something fresh. Sometimes, this requires taking a few steps back to unlearn.

Words and their meanings evolve over time. Take, for example, the word spirituality, derived from the Latin spiritus, meaning breath or spirit. In its early usage, spirituality was closely associated with religious devotion and the "breath of life" as a metaphor for divine presence. Over time, however, the concept expanded beyond religious confines, coming to represent personal growth, self-discovery, and a connection to something greater than oneself. Today, spirituality encompasses a sense of inner peace, personal development, and the search for meaning and purpose in life, transcending traditional religious frameworks.

> Science, is in the search of truth. Art has something to do with the gestalt. It is in our experiencing and expressing the truth.

Language can be intricate. To gain a deeper understanding and broader perspective, one must remain vigilant about what has already been learnt. It is essential to pause, take a step back, and examine whether any overlooked aspects exist. This interplay between knowledge and unlearning is both a science and an art.

Science takes the approach of dissection. It employs an analytical approach, breaking down complex subjects into smaller components to study them individually. The path of dissection is never ending and there is always something new to be discovered. Scientists identified the atom as the basic building block of matter. Further research revealed that atoms are composed of subatomic particles: electrons, protons, and neutrons. Further research led to discovery of fundamental particles. Many deeper questions remain and the dissection continues.

While science dissects reality to understand individual components, it also aims to integrate these insights into a unified whole. This integrative, intuitive grasp of complexity and interconnectedness – especially when it involves creativity and perception – aligns more closely with what we call Art. Art has something to do with the gestalt. We engage with the world through intuition, synthesis, creative insight and self-expression.

A scientist sees the world through a lens of precision, clarity, and empirical observation. An artist's eyes are attuned to colors, shapes, and the interplay of light and shadow. A painter for example, perceives the world through a lens of aesthetic sensitivity, emotion, and visual expression. A poet perceives the world through the lens of symbolism, metaphor, and emotional depth. They see beyond the surface, seeking deeper meanings in the nuances of life. Each perspective enriches our overall understanding of the world, contributing a unique dimension to the diverse human experience.

In the process of self-discovery, you must embody a scientist as well as an artist. Too much of a scientist, and you will miss the gestalt. Too much of an artist, you may be lost in emotions, the creativity and imagination to see that which is obvious for a scientist. Additionally, it is essential to be mindful of the nuances of language; becoming overly attached to words and knowledge can make you a scholar.

On the path of self-discovery, it is easy to get sidetracked and lose focus. This is not a journey of becoming. This is not of becoming a scientist, or an artist or a scholar or becoming someone else. This is a journey of being.

> Perspectives enrich our overall understanding.

The journey of being is an exploration and unfolding of one's authentic self. It involves a deep dive into the essence of who you are, embracing your true nature without the pressure to conform to external expectations or predefined roles. This journey encourages the exploration of your innermost thoughts, emotions, values, and aspirations.

This journey is about understanding your unique strengths, acknowledging your vulnerabilities, and fostering self-acceptance. It invites you to be present in the moment, appreciating the richness of your experiences while cultivating awareness. The journey is continuous and dynamic, allowing for growth, change, and self-discovery throughout life.

Along the way, you may explore various aspects of your identity, relationships, and connection to the world. It involves listening to your inner voice, recognizing patterns of thought and behavior, and discovering your core values. This path toward self-awareness and authenticity encourages you to embrace your true self rather than seek external validation or mold oneself to societal expectations.

Ultimately, it is about expressing yourself within the fabric of your unique existence – a journey of witnessing and being a witness.

Chapter Five

Silence

"Observe Silence."

Chapter Six

Polishing the tile

"Silence is not an absence,
But a presence – the presence of clarity."

A story from China – Mazu Daoyi was a student of the famous Chan master Nanyue Huairang. Mazu practiced meditation for more than a decade. Nanyue once visited Mazu and asked, "What are you doing these days?". Mazu said, "I have been sitting in meditation."

Nanyue asked, "What is your intention in sitting?" Mazu replied, "to become a Buddha."

Master Nanyue then picked up a tile and started polishing it. Mazu looking at Nanyue's expression said, "Master, what are you doing?" Nanyue replied, "Can't you see I am Polishing a tile?"

Mazu continued, "Why are you polishing?" for which the master replied, "I am trying to make a mirror out of the tile."
Mazu asked, "How is it possible to make a mirror by polishing the tile?" For which Nanyue remarked, "How can you do meditation and become a buddha?"
Mazu inquired, "Then, how so?"
For which Nanyue asked, "When driving a cart, if it stops moving, do you whip the cart or the ox?"
Listening to the Masters words, Mazu became silent.

> Practice of Stillness involves being aware of your posture, breathing and attitude.

We engage in practices like meditation and mindfulness with the expectation that they will help us navigate difficult times and facilitate the smooth pursuit of our worldly ambitions. Our inner voice nudges us to meditate, suggesting that it will provide just enough energy to keep up with life's struggles. We often set goals around achieving Stillness, treating it as a means to an end. Some aim to become a Buddha, while others chase the merits they believe will ease their afterlife. Many seek instant inner peace, while others want to wash away their sins or look for acquiring mystical powers.

A student once asked his teacher how long it would take to attain enlightenment if he meditated for two hours daily. The teacher replied, "Ten years." Then the student inquired if four hours of daily meditation would reduce that time, the teacher responded, "It will take you Fifty years." Hearing this the student was understandably frustrated.

The mind tends to be overly calculative, always seeking benefits. This transactional mindset can lead us to view life as a series of calculations, scrutinizing every action for its payoff. Ten years may seem like an eternity to the student, yet we rarely question the twenty-five years or more we spend accumulating degrees to graduate. We translate those years into prospective jobs and salaries, convincing ourselves that the wait is worth it. In contrast, the prospect of practicing Stillness for ten years can feel meaningless, as our minds struggle to perceive its value.

In the practice of Stillness, there is no goal, no intent, no becoming. You are it, just be.

Practice of Stillness: The Method

1. Be a witness to your Posture
2. Be a witness to your Breathing
3. Be a witness to your Attitude

Chapter Seven

Posture

"Stillness is not the absence of movement,
But the presence of awareness."

Whatever we engage in reveals something about us. By observing how our bodies position themselves, we can gain insight into our state of mind. Our state of being is reflected in our posture.

When we are happy and joyful, our bodies tend to be open and expansive. Conversely, when we feel sad or depressed, our bodies naturally adopt a closed posture – arms clasped around our legs, heads bowed, and eyes shut. In moments of worry or deep thought, we might rest our faces in our palms. A confident person walks with an erect back, illustrating how the body follows the mind.

Conversely, the mind also follows the body. By simply altering your posture, you can shift your state of mind.

Thus, it is essential to pay attention to your body position, whether you are sitting or standing.

While practicing Stillness, to cultivate a supportive posture, consider the full or half lotus position, whichever feels more comfortable for you. In the full lotus, place your right foot on your left thigh and your left foot on your right thigh. For the half lotus, position your left foot beneath the base of your right thigh and rest your right foot over your left thigh. Use a cushion to support your spine, ensuring that your knees rest comfortably on the ground and your spine remains erect. Strive to keep your body straight, avoiding any leaning to the sides or front.

> Our posture reflects our state of awareness. Be still in your posture.

Relax your shoulders and rest your hands freely, bringing your palms together – right palm below the left. Ensure your ears align with your shoulders and your nose points toward your navel. Keep your neck straight, with your chin slightly tucked in to maintain an upright posture. Close your eyes, focusing gently on the space between your eyebrows.

Be aware of your posture. It is natural to occasionally lose awareness of it, especially when thoughts begin to surface. When you become aware, recognize that you had lost awareness. This recognition of unawareness is a significant progress. Gently re-establish the right posture and continue your practice.

Chapter Eight

Breathing

"Breath connects the body and mind"

Imagine you are driving at a good speed, feeling the thrill of the moment but unaware of the risks involved. Only when you glance at the speedometer do you realize how fast you are traveling. This awareness empowers you to take control. Without which, the momentum from acceleration could throw you off course. The speedometer itself does not apply the brakes; instead, it prompts you to recognize that your rate of acceleration may be dangerous, urging you to reduce your speed to regain control. How often do you check the speedometer while driving?

Now, consider how often you observe your breath. Most of the time, we are unconscious of our breathing. Nature has designed a kind of speedometer within us, but we must be observant. Your breath functions as a speedometer, along with fulfilling many other purposes.

Breathing is intricately connected to health and longevity. For instance, a dog breathes rapidly, averaging 15-30 breaths per minute, while a tortoise breathes slowly, with an average of four breaths per minute. Interestingly, a dog's lifespan is typically 10-15 years, whereas a tortoise can live for 150 years or more.

> When you are worried, afraid or anxious, your mind is in a state of imbalance. Pay attention to your breath.

When you engage in strenuous activities, your breath quickens to supply your body with more oxygen. Notice how your breathing rate increases while running; even after you stop, you continue to breathe quickly until your breath normalizes. To recover from intense exertion, you might take deep breaths, helping your body return to a state of rest. This illustrates how our body regulates itself through breath. Athletes and individuals involved in physical activities understand the importance of breath and its impact on performance. Martial artists, meditators, yoga practitioners and practitioners of Tai Chi or Kungfu all train to cultivate breath awareness.

Breath control is also crucial for musicians. When listening to melodious tunes, you may find your breathing pattern shifts to align with the music. Conversely, harsh sounds can disturb your mind, reflecting in your breath.

Under normal resting conditions, we breathe at a rate of 12-20 breaths per minute. However, when experiencing fear, anger, agitation, or anxiety, our breathing speeds up. In states of worry, depression, or sadness, your breath may become irregular. During stress, you might find yourself exhaling audibly, releasing built-up tension. Physical activity is an effective way to combat stress, depression, and sadness.

When worried or anxious, your mind can become imbalanced, impairing your ability to listen and make sound decisions, which can lead to poor judgment. To regain balance, regulating your breath becomes essential. The mind follows the breath; breath serves as the bridge connecting our physical and psychological dimensions.

As we become attentive to our breath, we may differentiate breathing-in and breathing-out. In and out, are the boundaries we have defined between our Self and the outside world. The 'I' in us is continuously differentiating the inner, the outer, the body and the universe. This is the chatter of the mind.

In your practice of Stillness, avoid forcing your breath or attempting to slow it down. Simply allow it to flow naturally. Be a witness to your breath. There is nothing to be done; the approach is to be authentic. There are no techniques – just be as you are and follow your breath as it is. It will regulate itself.

Think of yourself as a door swinging open and closed, allowing air to enter as you inhale and exit as you exhale.

Inhale and exhale.
Inhale and exhale.
Inhale and exhale.
Inhale and exhale.

Follow the rhythm of your breath and become fully present to it. Allow this movement to exist, and nothing else. As you focus on your breath in this manner, your mind transitions from an agitated state to a more peaceful and relaxed one. With continued practice, you may eventually reach a state where only inhalation and exhalation exist – no body, no mind – just pure awareness of breathing.

As you begin your practice, there may be times when you might lose awareness of your breath due to distractions from thoughts or your physical environment. Recognize and acknowledge these moments where you have lost awareness. This realization is significant in your progress. Gently return your focus to the movement of your breath once again and continue to be a witness.

Chapter Nine

Attitude

"Stillness is nothing to get excited about"

An old master was in meditation near by the river. A young student approached him and said, "Master, I want to become your student, please teach me meditation". The master opened his eyes and asked, "Why do you want to learn meditation?" The student said, "I want to become enlightened."

The master reached out and caught hold of the student's collar, pulled him near, and then he held the student's neck from the back. Before the student could realize what was happening to him, in a flash, the old master plunged the student's head into the river. The student was in a state of shock, not knowing how to react in the situation. The student was trying hard to get out of the grip of the master. He was fighting for life unable to breathe as his face was under water. The master held the students head for a full minute inside the river before bringing him out. The master asked him "Now, tell me, what were you desiring the most underwater?" The student said, "I wanted air". The master said, "Very well then, come and see me when you want enlightenment as bad as you wanted air."

Here the master may seem to be harsh with the student, but the story points us to question how strong is our thirst for knowing the Self? Many a time we seek only out of curiosity. We are not invested in our question or our search. On the other hand, the mind is constantly on the lookout for benefits. While practice of Stillness can indeed act as a medicine, it is not a remedy you can simply pick up over the counter for immediate results. The desire to gain something is deeply ingrained in us, making it difficult for many to accept, adapt, or change without a clear payoff.

One day Raja saw a crowd starting to gather near the village lake. The village tax collector had fallen in to the lake and was calling for help. It was a bit deep, where he had fallen. The crowd around the tax collector ware trying to help, they said to the tax collector, "Give us your hand, Give us your hand! And we shall pull you out" But the tax collector didn't pay attention to the help being offered to rescue him. He kept on struggling in the water and crying for help. It was strange, the villagers were confused as to why this man was not giving his hand when offered and why is he simply crying for help. Raja came forward and said, "I will deal with this man." He stretched out his hand and shouted, "Dear Sir, Take my hand!" The tax collector instantly grabbed Raja's hand and was pulled out of the lake.

This is what happens – even when the tax collector is struggling with his life, he only understands the language of 'take'. This language of acquiring something has become a hindrance.

Your attitude should not be to gain something from doing the practice. To gain is not the goal. Stillness is not a goal. It merely facilitates in expressing your original nature. One cannot make a goal out of it. When you practice Stillness, set aside all the engagements of the world. Do not be distracted by the dualities of good and bad, right and wrong. Do not be concerned of goals, of time and of virtues.

As your practice in Stillness matures, you may observe improvements to your mental and physical health. These are the side effects or by-products of practice. One should not practice Stillness in pursuit of them.

If our attitude is right, we can observe the right posture and breathing.

In the context of an organization, everyone follows the head of the organization. If the head is right, everyone in the organization will function right. If the head is not organized in thought and conduct, the organization will not function efficiently. Similarly, if our attitude is right, we can observe the right posture and breathing. If our attitude is not right, then it will reflect in our posture and breathing.

Bring awareness to your attitude and be a witness.

Chapter Ten

Beginner's mind

"Silence is not empty;
It is full of possibilities."

Nan-in, a Japanese master, received a university professor who came to inquire about Zen. Nan-in served tea. He poured his visitor's cup full and then kept on pouring.

The professor watched the overflow until he no longer could restrain himself from saying. "It is overflowing. The cup is full. No more will go in!"

"Like this cup," Nan-in said, "you are full of your own opinions and speculations. How can I speak of Zen unless you first empty your cup?"

The university professor was a knowledgeable man. The master recognized that he did not come to inquire about Zen. The professor had come to test the master. So, the master responded to the situation. If the professor knew the taste of Zen, he would have immediately recognized the master's response. The professor's mind was filled with all the knowledge about Zen. He has been acquiring it over many years. He did not have room to taste the master's wisdom.

The essence of Stillness is in witnessing and it cannot be transmitted through words. 'Beginner's mind' refers to having an attitude of openness, eagerness, and lack of preconceptions when approaching a subject, just as a beginner would do. You approach it with a sense of curiosity and a willingness to explore it from all aspects without prejudice. Having a beginner's mind means you are receptive to new ideas, open to feedback, and eager to learn. It is a mindset that fosters continuous personal and intellectual growth.

> The usefulness of a cup is in its emptiness. Empty your cup.

In the beginning, there is nothing, but as you acquire knowledge, you lose the beginner's mind. You are no longer a beginner, as you start to cling around knowledge. You start viewing everything through the lens of what you've learnt. This perspective is natural, and there's nothing inherently wrong with it. However, when you become fixated on what you know, you close yourself from the inside. This is when challenges arise: you become filled with opinions and prejudices. This is the downside of knowledge acquisition. Your attention becomes selective, limiting your ability to truly listen and observe. Information is filtered, and you only take in what aligns with your preconceptions. To have an empty mind is to have the mind of a beginner.

An old Chinese proverb – '*The usefulness of a cup is in its emptiness*'. In the kitchen, when you have an empty container, the container is ready to use, it has the capacity to hold something. But if the container is full, you look for a new container that is empty, or you clean the container so that it can be reused. If suppose the container is half filled, anything you add to it loses its originality. When you are empty, a master can pour his wisdom into you. He can transform you.

Having a beginner's mind involves suspending judgment. Withhold from criticizing and evaluating until you have fully explored and understood a subject or situation. By being fully present in the moment and paying attention to your experiences without bias or judgment, you can cultivate a more open and receptive mindset. It is a reminder – to approach life with the enthusiasm and curiosity of a beginner, even as you accumulate knowledge and experience over time.

MUDDY WATERS

Chapter Eleven

The mask

"In the stillness, the ego quiets,
And the true Self emerges."

The word personality is derived from the Greek word persona, meaning a mask used by actors in Greek drama. When you are born, you have no identity. You are a clean slate. As you are introduced to the world, a gender, name, religion, caste, and nationality are assigned to you; these become part of your identity. However, this identity is shaped from the outside. Once enveloped in these identifiers, you begin to claim them as your own, as if they were inherent. It is important to remember that all these identities are given to you and you have borrowed it.

For instance, if people around you call you beautiful, you may adopt this view as a core part of your identity. Now, you perceive the world through this borrowed identity. It is borrowed because it consists of opinions from others, which you have accumulated. If someone challenges this, saying you are not beautiful, it can threaten your sense of identity, as this identity is external and therefore fragile.

As you grow, your experiences shape your beliefs, emotions, and thoughts, further solidifying your identifications. Over time, these identifications become stronger, deeply embedded constructs that shape your worldview. Due to these accumulated identities and environmental conditioning, you perceive the world through a particular lens, which appears as your reality – but this is a pseudo-reality. Had your experiences been different, your worldview would likely be different as well.

We often interpret the world from the vantage point of our self-imposed identifications. For example, a doctor who is strongly identified with his profession may behave as a doctor not only at work but also among friends, family, or in other contexts. This professional identity begins to overshadow the real person beneath it.

The Japanese have a saying that '*each person has three faces: the first shown to the world, the second to family and friends, and the third kept hidden from everyone.*' This third face is the unmasked Self, buried beneath layers of personality and ego.

This is personality engulfing you. This is what we call Ego. When you function from a specific identification, you are said to have Ego. This becomes your false center from where you function.

Ego manifests in various forms and identities. It is a multiplicity yet we often address it as a singular phenomenon. It is so close to you that it can be hard to recognize. Much like standing close to a glass window, where the glass eventually seems to disappear, you may need some distance to truly see it. Similarly, you are so closely identified with aspects of yourself that stepping back becomes essential to recognize these identifications. This process involves witnessing and becoming aware of your false centers.

A king was known for his humble nature. Everybody in his kingdom praised him, that even after being such a great king, he has no ego. Despite of all the victories in wars, and all the wealth and riches he possesses, he stays so humble.

One day, the king was visiting a temple to offer prayers. It so happened that a poor man was also in the temple that morning, offering his prayers. The king overheard the poor man in prayer saying, "I am your most humble servant". Hearing this, the king became furious, filled with anger and rage.

> If there is a sense of 'I' in your thoughts, speech and action, there is Ego. Any form of attention is food for the Ego.

As we can see, this reaction from a king is predictable. How could anyone dare to claim they were humbler than the king? The situation had turned into a competition of humility. The king's humbleness was a performance, an act, not a genuine expression. When humility itself becomes a goal, this is often the result: the ego wants to secure the title of "most humble." Some people act humble, hoping others will notice and admire their modesty, wanting people to think, "Look how humble this person is."

The games of the ego are many. Ego can thrive on material possessions, education, achievements, wealth, success, and status. It can also thrive on love, compassion, sacrifice, humility, and piety. As the ego becomes subtler, it becomes increasingly difficult to detect. Any form of attention feeds it. Obvious displays of ego are easy to spot, but as it becomes more refined and concealed, recognizing its presence requires deeper awareness. If there is a sense of 'I' in your thoughts, speech and action, recognize that there is Ego. Any form of attention is food for the Ego.

In your Stillness, observe your identifications, and how it has shaped your personality. Be a witness.

Chapter Twelve

The begging bowl

"Stillness does not extinguish desire;
It clarifies what is truly worth pursuing."

What is the nature of desire? Our mind is full of wants and desires. When one desire is fulfilled, the mind moves on to pursue the next desire. Mind is continuously in movement and in this pursuit of desires, mind is never at ease.

A part of you is hankering for the past that is lost, and another part of you is pulled towards the imagined future. You are attracted by desires and you want to become many things all at the same time. In this pursuit of gratification, you lose sight of yourself. It seems like we are in a race against time. Pause and reflect – where is this race truly taking you? Mind never seems to find fulfillment. In fact, desire and mind are not two separate words. Mind is desire.

A man dreamt of owning a car for the comfort of his family. He desired it, longed for it, and then one day there it was his dream car in his parking lot. The day he got his car delivered; he came out excited to receive it, but there stood another new car next to his, a much bigger and luxurious car which was newly purchased by his neighbor. Immediately the excitement and happiness of having finally purchased his new car disappeared. He started dreaming about purchasing a better car than his neighbor. He was finished with all his longing and desire for the car he purchased. His desire had already moved.

Observe that desire cannot live in what is available to you. Desire just drives you from one point to another. Desire is the endless game of the mind. The object of desire is irrelevant, any desire would do. Desire of things, power, respect, or the desire to go to heaven or something spiritual. You are always in the grip of desire. This is a very unconscious state. Hence the suffering. Many have renounced the world. They have moved to mountains and monasteries, but they remain the same. Earlier they were desiring for comforts, luxuries, success in the world. When they experienced failures, boredom or dissatisfaction, the mind suggests "let us try in the opposite direction", and now they are in pursuit of the other worldly goals of spirituality – enlightenment and nirvana.

Have you observed that we tend to move in opposite directions? Children want to act like adults, while adults want to become children again. When you are surrounded by noise, you seek solitude, and when you have solitude, you seek company. Those who are single are looking to get married and those in marriage are looking to go single. This is the irony of life. The love affair is finished as soon as one gets married. The love affair is in the pursuit. Desire is alive in your dreaming of the future, your wait and anticipations of the future. Desire is never in the present. It is always of the future. It ceases to exist in the present.

By nature, desire is unfulfillable. It is a never-ending chase. When you accomplish one desire, the desire is no longer relevant, you are finished with it. Mind never rests, as it is always in the look out to pursue. It is important to take a closer look at how our mind and desire functions and what this movement is doing to us. What is our mind moving away from? What is it moving towards? It is said that '*desire is the root cause of suffering*', and it is in this context that desire becomes the root cause of suffering.

> This idea to renounce something, is from the stand point of desire being seen as something bad.

When we say suffering, the intensity of it is felt differently by each individual based on what suffering means to them. The experience is very subjective. Our emotional investment is directly proportional to intensity of our suffering, ranging from something brief to something deeply impactful. Let us give a simpler definition to the word suffering such as – our mind is uneasy. The degree of uneasiness can vary between something small or something very big. So, if desire is the cause of all suffering (the uneasiness of the mind), should you renounce desire? Pause and reflect on this aspect.

The idea is not about renouncing the desire, this does not help in your path of self-discovery. It is not a matter of taking sides - for or against. It is not the right approach. In your practice of Stillness, you do not want to go for or against something. If you try to renounce or do away with, this is not right understanding.

We are a living system driven by energy. Both the physical and psychological aspects consume this energy to sustain life. You the Self, are capable of channeling the energy in the direction you desire. But the question is are you channeling the energy, so that you can function in the most efficient way as a system – or – the energies are on auto pilot, doing their own thing and you remain at their mercy.

Fundamental nature, such as 'to desire' is a capability that life has bestowed upon you. You are capable of desiring; This is something significant. You cannot renounce it, as it is part of you. Many schools of thought want you to renounce desire, but is it really possible? You just end up wasting time trying to renounce. This idea to renounce something, is from the stand point of desire being seen as a hindrance or something bad, and that is why you are asked to renounce desire. In the process of disciplining, you start to suppress desire. Suppression is not the same as being in control. It often backfires. These buried impulses may resurface with greater force, manifesting as compulsions, mood swings, anxiety, or even psychosomatic symptoms. What you resist, persists. Suppressed desires, when not acknowledged and consciously worked through, tend to erupt in unpredictable and often destructive ways through addictions, emotional outbursts, or displaced behavior. This rebound effect occurs because the Self seeks expression and integration, not denial.

Let us suppose you start suppressing as a way of self-disciplining yourself and in this process, if your desire resurfaces, it leads you to feeling guilty. When you experience guilt, mind is always in conflict and you are always in a grip of control. You feel your practice is not good because you are unable to overcome desires. This guilt is a psychological trap. Guilt keeps you at war with yourself. With such disciplining, you are always trying to move away from what life has given you. How can you find peace if you are always at war with yourself? In the process of such disciplining, you are moving further away from discovering your Self.

The practice of Stillness is concerned with your understanding of the fundamental nature. What nature has provided to you, you can only accept. Embrace yourself as you are, including the desires that arise within. Be a witness to what unfolds inside you as these desires emerge.

As your understanding of the cyclical nature of desire deepens, desire naturally loses relevance. You reach a point where there is nothing left to renounce, requiring no effort to let go – it simply falls away. Just as a ripe fruit falls off a tree branch without any effort, so does a desire when seen for its futility. When you have truly lived through an emotion or desire and recognize its transience, release happens effortlessly. In an act of witnessing, the desire falls away on its own, and you experience freedom.

One morning, a beggar encountered a king outside the palace. The king asked him, "What do you want?". It was customary that the king never denies anyone early in the morning and always provides what is asked by his subjects. The beggar laughed. He said, "You are asking as if you can fulfill my desire! Now you tell me, what do you want?"

The king was very offended, he felt challenged. He said, "You have dared to be rude and have challenged my capacity. You have risked your life in doing so. But today is your lucky day, I will spare your ignorance. Tell me what you want. I am your king and will fulfill your wishes."

And the man said, "Think twice before you promise anything."

King said, "Before your luck runs out and you annoy me anymore, just tell me what you want and I will fulfill it."

The beggar brought out a begging bowl from his bag. And the beggar said, "You see this begging bowl? Can you fill it with something? Anything will do."

King said, "You seem to be unintelligent; you could have asked for anything, but you are asking me to fill this small bowl." He called one of his ministers and told him, "Fill this man's begging bowl with gold coins."

The minister filled the bowl with gold coins, and soon the gold disappeared. The minister poured more gold and everything he put in disappeared. The bowl remained empty. The king was starting to worry. The news soon spread life fire and crowd started to gather.

The king's ego was hurt even more. He said to his minister, "I am ready to even lose my kingdom, but I cannot be defeated by this beggar. I have to prove that I can fill this bowl."

His treasuries started becoming empty. Just about everything disappeared. Diamonds, pearls, and emeralds, everything disappeared. The minister suggested the king to accept defeat, as it seems like he is no ordinary beggar.

The king realized the situation and bowed down to the beggar and said, "Dear sir, I accept my defeat. I realize you are no ordinary beggar. You have not crossed my path to ask me to fill this bowl. It seems that you are carrying a message for me. What is a secret to this begging bowl? Please help me understand"

The beggar said, "Oh King! this bowl has no magic. It is simply made from the human skull I found at the graveyard. There is no secret in it. This is how the mind functions." Saying these words, the beggar disappeared.

Chapter Thirteen

Black-nosed Buddha

"In Stillness we see past the barriers of our own limited thinking,
And open up our small mind."

A Zen nun who was in search of enlightenment, worshiped a statue of golden buddha. Wherever she went, she would carry this golden buddha with her. Years passed, and the nun came to live in a small temple where there were many other buddha statues of other monks. The nun wished to burn incense before her golden buddha. Not liking the idea of the perfume straying to other's buddha statues, she devised a funnel through which the smoke would ascend only to her statue. This blackened the nose of the golden buddha.

Due to our ego, one is inherently possessive and selfish; it seeks only which benefits itself, leaving little room for sharing or consideration of others. Here even

Buddha is not spared. He is divided into her Buddha and other's Buddha. This is the small mind – the ego. Forget about the search for enlightenment, just the idea that the incense aroma has to reach to only her Buddha's nose, is absurd. But this is what happens. It is necessary to pause and reflect on what are you clinging to, even in your practice? Our attachments extends beyond our material possessions. We would not even spare the divine. One becomes greedy. Greed is not just about money or things, it encompasses power, attention, and affection. In this case, even the Buddha.

> Pay attention to what is happening inside you and how the energy is manifesting

Desire is fundamental. When your stomach is empty and you feel hunger, your body signals the need for nourishment, prompting you to seek food to restore energy balance and relieve that emptiness. This is a biological need. Desire also extends beyond just the physical need and we experience psychological hunger and we start to desire even more and fill beyond what is needed. This is the nature of greed – your energy moves into greed as your compulsiveness to acquire increases.

When a desire arises within you and remains unfulfilled, it creates restlessness in the heart. If another holds what you long for, the energy, clouded by comparison, moves into jealousy. This jealousy does not ease the desire; it sharpens it moving you towards desperation.

From jealousy, you move into anger. Your energy, which could have been directed inward toward understanding, turns outward into agitation. You begin to burn, not because of the other's possession, but because you cannot accept your own feeling of emptiness.

If wisdom does not intervene, anger moves into hatred. You may not hate the person, but you begin to resent the world. Life feels unfair. Joy in others becomes pain in you.

This is the shadow of desire left unchecked; it closes the heart, narrows the mind, and binds your spirit. You begin to live not from your center, but from the restless edge of comparison.

No one truly owns anything. All things arise, and all things pass. The moment you turn within and see the root of desire, not as something to be fulfilled, but as something to be understood, a great shift occurs. The energy that once moved as craving becomes awareness. And in awareness, peace begins. As we grow, one should aspire to become better, not bitter.

When your friends excel in studies while you do not, you may feel unhappy. If someone gets a job while you are still unable to land one, your unhappiness can deepen. Your colleague's success may breed discontent, and your neighbor's prosperity can spark feelings of inadequacy. The root of this unhappiness often lies in the desire to be the first to achieve.

By paying attention to your internal state and how your energy manifests, you can transform it into something positive. The energy is the same, but how you direct it reflects your inner self. You can choose to move into anger and hatred or embrace joy and love.

Hunger is cyclical in nature. It can never be truly satisfied. When you feel hungry, you seek food, but soon after, the hunger returns. The same applies to thirst; drinking water temporarily suppresses it, only for it to resurface. On the other hand, fasting often heightens thoughts of food, making it clear that suppressing hunger only amplifies it. Those who overeat may think about fasting, but when they do, thoughts of food dominate their minds. Once the period of fast is completed you may find yourself indulging in binge eating. This cycle is similar to how our desires keep reappearing, prompting us to pursue gratification constantly.

Have you noticed that genuinely happy people seem less hungry? Children exemplify this; they often radiate joy and are not fixated on food, yet they maintain abundant energy throughout the day. Oftcn it so happens that you do not experience hunger in moment s of joy, for example when you are hosting a celebration; during those times, hunger often fades into the background. On the contrary, sadness can lead to increased eating.

When you are happy, your joy overflows. You are compelled to share that happiness due to the overflowing of joy. You experience an openness within. During moments of sadness, you feel closed.

Everyone wants to be happy. In this pursuit of happiness, you are unknowingly also choosing your unhappiness. Where ever there is happiness, like a shadow, there is bound to be unhappiness as well. This constant pursuit of happiness often leads us to unhappiness, resulting in a cycle of suffering.

When you begin to witness the endless chase to fulfill your desires, a quiet shift occurs. You no longer move blindly, caught in the current of craving. Instead, you start to see the futility of the chase. In this witnessing, something deeper awakens.

You are no longer pulled by the hope of fulfillment. You begin to rest, not in what you want, but in what is. The restless striving gives way to Stillness. A different realm opens within you, not of achievement, but of alignment; Not of craving, but of harmony.

This is the beginning of freedom when you stop reaching outward, and begin abiding in the truth that nothing is missing. Contentment represents a state of inner harmony, where you are at peace with yourself and the world. In this state, your mind is clear, your heart is light, and your spirit is spacious enough to embrace the entire world. A content person remains unaffected by desire; they may desire something, but if it happens, they are okay with it; if not, they are still okay. Ultimately, 'being okay' is what truly matters.

Chapter Fourteen

Peeling onion

"In silence, we uncover the layers of our true being."

Thoughts are the building blocks of who we are and how we function. We are exposed to many kinds of stimuli during our journey in life. In the process we learn and form impressions. The accumulated experiences, beliefs, and societal influences, along with the memories and associated feelings, form the many layers of conditioning.

Conditioning is a form of learning. To understand the Self, we must uncover the many layers of conditioning to which we have been subjected to. Imagine an onion. Each layer represents a certain mental construct affecting the Self.

Society plays an important role in how we are conditioned. Our thoughts, speech, and actions are influenced by the beliefs, ideologies, and moral values instilled in us. These elements form the limits or boundaries within which we function. We acquire them from the outside and internalize them, making them an integral part of who we are.

A group of scientists placed five monkeys in an enclosed cage with a ladder in the middle of the cage and on top of the ladder, they placed a few bananas. Every time a monkey went up the ladder, the other monkeys were soaked up in cold water. After a while, every time a monkey attempted to go up the ladder, the other monkeys beat up the one who tried to go up the ladder.

This went on for a while and the monkeys had learned that whenever they beat up the monkey climbing the ladder, there was no cold water. Slowly, the monkeys in the cage were replaced one after the other by the scientists. Over a period of time, none of the original five monkeys were in the cage. All the new monkeys had learnt something from the other but have never experienced the spraying of cold water. There were no bananas as well on the ladder. But monkeys are monkeys, if they find a ladder, they will attempt to climb. Every time any monkey would climb, the others would start beating up the one trying to climb the ladder. The new set of monkeys have no idea why they beat up the one trying to climb the ladder in the first place. This is how conditioning works leading to blind practices.

In your practice of Stillness, reflect on your conditioning and how it has shaped you.

> Emotions are who we are. They are our super powers.

Our mental conditioning is reflected in our body language. Our eyes see only what we are permitted to see. In certain cultures, direct eye contact is considered rude. Similarly, we listen only if we are allowed to listen, and we eat only if we are given permission to eat. Many cultures have established gender roles and expectations that dictate how individuals are supposed to behave. We act in ways that our conditioning approves of, which is a form of compliance. This moral policing occurs within our minds.

Our thoughts often engage us in a dialogue about what is good and bad, right and wrong. It is important to observe the conditionings that have taken shape within us. Our obsession with upholding what we have learned defines our rigidity or flexibility. When we are too fixated and rigid, it becomes a barrier to fully experiencing life.

Galileo, the famous Italian astronomer and physicist, said that the Earth revolves around the Sun. He was punished to have made those claims and was forced to say that the Sun revolves around the Earth as that was the belief. He was house arrested until death for having the view that the Earth revolves around the Sun. Such is the affairs of collective beliefs.

Observe your borrowed beliefs, your borrowed ideologies and your borrowed morals. Go deep into them as they affect your reason and rationalization. Due to our conditioned mental constructs, we often see the world in a very biased way. Our response to life situations lacks clarity in decisions and thought. It is one thing to live by certain rules of the society and it is another, when the rules starts living through you. Then you become only a means for the existence of rigid ideologies and beliefs. Take time to contemplate this notion.

Next, we encounter the layer of our identifications, our attachments – our Ego. Ego is our false center. Both conditioning and the Ego are outer layers that act as filters for how we perceive the world; It is a construct born of identification and separation, constantly trying to protect its version of 'me' or 'mine.' Due to this we subject ourselves to confirmation bias. Even on the spiritual path, this subtle distortion persists. A seeker may read scriptures, not to awaken, but to confirm what they already think is true. They may listen to a teacher, not to be transformed, but to be reassured. In this way, the ego wears the robes of the seeker.

As we go deeper in Stillness, introspect on the layer of emotions. Emotions are who we are. They are our super powers. If we are not in a balanced state of emotion, it affects our thoughts, speech and actions. Skewed emotional states hinder our ability to reason. More often than not, the ego and conditioning manipulate emotions. Frequently, genuine emotions are suppressed. These suppressed emotions can take different forms and affect an individual in various ways. One major reason people suppress their emotions is the fear of vulnerability. In professional environments, for example, individuals may feel compelled to hide feelings of frustration, anger, or sadness to maintain a facade of professionalism. This fear is often rooted in the conditioning that associates emotional expression with weakness or instability. Consequently, individuals may resort to masking their true feelings, leading to a disconnect between their inner experiences and outward behavior. Moreover, societal norms often dictate how emotions should be expressed, further complicating the issue. For instance, men may be conditioned to view the expression of sadness or vulnerability as unmasculine, while women subjected to this social bias may be labeled as overly emotional if they express anger. This cultural conditioning can result in the internalization of the belief that certain emotions are unacceptable, compelling individuals to suppress their feelings rather than confront and express them. For instance, if someone wants to express their anger and are unable to, they may continue to suppress it, if there is no outlet for expression. There is a limit to how much suppression one can endure, and in the long run, it may impact both mental and physical health. Suppression of any kind is dangerous, as it will eventually resurface once it surpasses a threshold. Emotions are our 'life force seeking expression.' If we respect the power that emotions hold, they can do wonders for our well-being. Conversely, if we are careless with our emotions, they can be as destructive as ruining one's life. By acknowledging and expressing our emotions, we can foster a deeper connection with ourselves and others, promoting a more fulfilling and authentic life. Embracing our emotional experiences allows us to harness their power, leading to personal growth and healthier relationships. Go deep in your practice of Stillness to observe your emotions.

The next layer is our instincts. Instinct is part of human biology and evolution passed on from one generation to the next. They are hard wired behaviors that have evolved over time and are our automatic response essential for survival or self-preservation. The fight-or-flight response is a survival instinct triggered in response to perceived threats. It prepares the body to either confront or flee from danger, increasing the chances of survival in the face of physical or psychological stress. The sexual instinct ensures the continuation of the species; while nurturing and protective behaviors ensure the survival of the young. Social instincts that govern cooperation, group bonding, and social hierarchies, help individuals live and thrive in groups, which historically increased survival chances. Forming alliances, seeking social approval, and establishing leadership roles can be seen as manifestations of social instincts. Our instincts are also influenced and shaped by our conditioning. Due to conditioning, our natural instincts are corrupted. Instincts may also be suppressed due to reinforcements such as rewards or punishment. Cultural and societal norms and values can strongly influence how instincts are expressed. Our conformance to behavioral standards set by the society, family or organization and, our complex emotions, can affect how we express or repress these instincts. Observe how you are when no one is around you, and how you behave when you are among your colleagues, friends or family.

Repression of what is natural, causes imbalance. Repressed emotions can lead to blockages or imbalance in how we respond to life situations, disrupting the free flow of energy and potentially causing emotional issues or physical discomfort. Imbalances can lead to issues related to these instincts, such as fear, anxiety, insecurity, or excessive desire. Repressed anger leads to passive aggressive behavior which can affect your relationships, leading to increased stress, resentment and emotional imbalance. Repression of sexual desires can impact your mental health, relationship dynamics, and overall well-being. Repression of thoughts around existential questions of Self, life and death limits awareness and hinders personal growth. When individuals avoid confronting these profound inquiries, they may experience a sense of disconnection from their true selves and the world around them. This repression can lead to a lack of clarity about one's values, purpose, and identity, ultimately resulting in feelings of emptiness or dissatisfaction. All these contribute to the imbalance of the Self.

> Repression of what is natural, causes imbalance. Repression of emotions can lead to blockages or imbalance in how we respond to life situations.

Engaging with existential questions around Self, Life and Death is essential for fostering a deeper understanding of oneself, enhancing awareness, and promoting emotional well-being. By confronting and exploring these thoughts, you can cultivate a more authentic and fulfilling existence. Addressing and releasing repressions helps in balancing your emotions and promoting overall well-being. Doing so, you experience a greater sense of emotional and psychological harmony. As you become a witness in

Stillness to your instincts, emotions, and repressions, all imbalances will gradually dissolve on their own.

Then comes the layer of intuition. Intuition is our ability to understand something without the need for conscious reasoning. It is a form of implicit knowledge that plays a significant role in decision-making and problem-solving. While intuition may not be conditioned in the same way that learned behaviors are, it is certainly influenced by past experiences, knowledge, and conditioning. Thus, we can say that our intuitive faculty may not be fully active as a result of these factors. Intuition is linked to a deep state of relaxation. Many discoveries have been made through intuition during deep sleep. The great Indian mathematician, Ramanujam, was known to have the answers to the most difficult problems in mathematics, but he did not know how he arrived at them. He is said to have dreamt of it. This is our connectedness to the great intelligence of the universe. Discoveries of Periodic Table and the Benzene ring happened in a dream. You may have had the experience of some flashing moments of intuition. It may have so happened that you were working on solving a problem for long and are unable to solve it and then you drop all that you are doing and switch to some other activity totally unrelated to the problem, and suddenly the answer you were looking for earlier appears before you. You have a eureka moment. Intuition functions when one is relaxed and in a pure state of let go.

Chapter Fifteen

Deadly poisons

"Mind is restless;
Find peace in self-acceptance."

In your witnessing of emotions, you will come across two powerful emotions – guilt and regret. Twins of a certain nature, they always follow one another. Together they are capable of transforming or destroying life.

A couple lived happily with their six-year-old daughter and a newly born baby boy. One day, disaster struck their family. While no one was around, the baby fell off the cot onto the floor and died. It was tragic. Their life seemed destroyed by the death of their son. The wife felt guilt and was so deep in regret that she could not digest the fact that her child was no more. Their dreams were shattered. Together they could not handle the comments and criticism from their near and dear ones. Every day, there was nothing but sadness from this tragedy. On the outside they were also burdened to look normal, they had to muster the courage to move on from this phase of life. Life was difficult, in fact impossible. Eight months passed by. One morning, the news came that the wife killed her six-year-old daughter and she committed suicide. It got even more dramatic when the husband turned mad. Their happy-go, well-to-do family was destroyed.

> A rose flower is complete. A marigold is complete. A lotus is complete, But for the Man.

Regret and guilt consume all your energies. You are no longer able to do anything under the grip of guilt and regret. There is no other emotion that can ruin an individual's life like guilt and regret. It destroys one's self-image and self-respect.

The guilt and regret are also equally capable of transforming you.

A thief entered the house of a Zen master. The master was in meditation. The thief threatened the master with a knife saying, "give me all you have or I will have your head". The master replied, "do not disturb me, what you want is in the top drawer of the cupboard and you can have it". The thief was surprised by this response, but went ahead, took the money and left the house. A few days later, he was caught for another offence in the neighborhood, and in his submission, he also mentioned about the theft he had committed in the Zen master's house.

When asked about the theft, the Zen master said to the officials, "He did not steal any money. I gave it to him"

Hearing this, the thief felt regret for his actions and after serving his term in the Jail, he came to the Zen master and became his disciple.

What has the power to destroy also has the power to transform. The reason why one succumbs to emotions such as guilt and regret and how they negatively impact us so quickly is due to our conditioning. You have been conditioned to feel incomplete throughout your life. The feeling of incompleteness is a human experience, characterized by the sense that something essential is missing in one's life. This feeling can manifest across different dimensions – personal, social, emotional, or material – and it is deeply intertwined with self-perception and identity. This sense of incompleteness is influenced by a combination of internal factors, such as self-esteem and emotional regulation, as well as external forces, such as societal expectations and cultural conditioning. There is always something missing that you believe needs to be fulfilled. A smartphone, for instance; if everyone else has one, and you do not, then that makes you feel incomplete. Someone has good looks, and you feel incomplete because of your ordinary appearance, leading to a sense of insecurity and loss of confidence. This affects your self-esteem. Makeup then becomes necessary for you to feel confident and complete, masking your so-called shortcomings. Today, wearing makeup is the new norm, and those without access to it often live with a sense of incompleteness. You have spent your entire life chasing fulfillment, while there is no end to this pursuit.

This feeling of incompleteness is due to the habit of comparison. Our society significantly contributes in fostering the feeling of incompleteness. We are too busy constantly comparing and judging. This behavior is deeply ingrained making its way into everyone's subconscious. This further induces and strengthens inferiority and superiority complexes. Chronic feelings of incompleteness can have a profound impact on mental health, contributing to conditions such as anxiety, depression, and low self-esteem. When individuals are trapped in a state of perpetual dissatisfaction, they may struggle with a constant sense of failure or inadequacy. This emotional burden can lead to avoidance behaviors, where individuals withdraw from opportunities for growth or connection, fearing that they will never be enough. In addition, feeling incomplete can foster a reliance on external validation, leading people to seek approval from others rather than finding confidence within themselves. This dependence on external factors for self-worth can create a fragile sense of identity, easily shattered by criticism, rejection, or failure. Social media exacerbates this phenomenon by creating a platform for constant comparison. People often present an idealized version of their lives online, highlighting success, beauty, and happiness, while concealing struggles and imperfections. This can lead to a distorted sense of reality for those who consume this content, intensifying feelings of inadequacy or incompleteness as they believe they fall short of what others appear to have achieved. Consumer culture also fuels the notion of incompleteness. Advertisements are designed to make people feel as though their lives are lacking without a certain product or service. This perpetuates a cycle of wanting and acquiring, with the promise of fulfillment always just out of reach. The messaging is – happiness and completeness lie in external achievements, possessions, or status, but this external focus prevents people from finding lasting satisfaction within themselves.

To overcome this feeling of incompleteness, the mind looks for ways to compensate or substitute that which it perceives as lacking. This leads to a cycle of filling life with compensations, whether through material possessions, achievements, or external validation, in an attempt to cover up perceived shortcomings and feeling inferior. These compensations in reality are simply reinforcing the sense of inadequacy. Life cannot be lived to the fullest when you fill your moments with compensations for perceived shortcomings. By constantly seeking to mask what you believe is missing, you end up leading a false life, disconnected from your true self. Any amount of compensation does not satisfy your need for fulfillment. This effort to compensate is the mind's effort to protect the perceived self-image – your false identity. It is important to note that both inferiority and superiority complexes are arising out of this insecurity. The longer you support, the more you are invested in protecting this false image or identity. True fulfillment comes not from compensating for these insecurities, but from embracing who you are, without relying on external validation or artificial substitutes.

Look at a rose; it does not worry about its thorns – it blooms regardless. A blade of grass stands tall next to a bamboo shoot. A rose is complete, as is a marigold, a lotus, a blade of grass and everything else in nature. In your journey of self-discovery, reflect on what incompleteness means to you. Are there areas of life where you feel lacking? How did you acquire these feelings of incompleteness, of fear and insecurity?

The practice of Stillness helps you to focus on the present moment and to cultivate awareness of thoughts and emotions without judgment. It enables you to realize that you are 'complete' to start with, and this false sense of incompleteness you have been nurturing is simply the result of conditioning. In this realization, insecurity will no longer haunt you – it simply fades away.

AWAKENING

Chapter Sixteen

House on fire

"If you love a flower, water the plant."

It is said that Buddha renounced the world. But, did he really renounce the world?

When prince Siddhartha left home to become a ascetic, his father, king Suddhodana, became unhappy. Siddhartha's wife was unhappy that he left her and their son Rahula. The people of Kapila were unhappy by his decision. To some, it may have seemed like an abandonment of familial and royal duties. For those closest to him, it was a time marked by profound sadness.

Society tends to disapprove of someone who embodies true aliveness. A person who is fully alive is independent and stands apart from the crowd. If such a person does not conform to societal norms, they may be viewed as difficult to control or manage.

> When you realize that the stones you are carrying are not real diamonds, you drop them immediately, you don't need intelligence.

Society often discourages individuality, favoring conformity over personal expression. People who deviate from accepted norms or pursue their own unique paths face resistance or judgment, as social structures tend to prioritize uniformity and collective identity over individual freedom.

Rules and norms play a role in the functioning of society. Some rules are common sense, if you don't follow traffic rules, you may end up with an accident. Rules are necessary to reduce chaos and maintain a certain harmony in the community. A norm is an unwritten, informal standard of behavior that is socially expected within a group. It is not enforced by law but by social pressure or cultural conditioning. Norms at times are stifling when they discourage individuals from expressing themselves. When the original reason for the existence of a norm no longer exists, we may be holding on to outdated norms rigidly, impacting progress or change. For example, people may stay silent in the face of injustice just because "that's how things are." Over time, we internalize social norms so deeply that we begin to limit ourselves.

A husband never feels free when his wife is around. Likewise, the wife may have the similar feeling. Although neither of them are interfering with each other. A child may also feel restricted when parents are around. Why is this feeling of restriction? If everyone is loving, then shouldn't love elevate one another to a sense of freedom? Deep down, we engage in a subtle form of manipulation. The love we express is often utilitarian, an exchange for something, leading to this uncomfortable feeling. Reflect on what is it that we experience as love?

Siddhartha was no ordinary individual; he was born into a royal family. There was a prophecy that he would take the spiritual path and become a spiritual leader or he would become a great king. Hearing the prophecy, the king was deeply concerned and worried about Siddhartha's future and the future of the kingdom. He was worried that Siddhartha might choose the spiritual path and renounce the throne. He consulted the wise men of his court on how the boy can be kept away from taking the spiritual path. The king was advised by the seers and wise men to fill Siddhartha's life with luxuries and keep him away from all pain and suffering. In retrospect, the wise men were not so wise after all. They probably projected their own short comings in life, only to suggest the king that if Siddhartha lived among all luxuries, he would not choose the spiritual path. As per the advice, the king kept Siddhartha within the confines of the palace, surrounding him with luxury, pleasure, and beauty. In an effort to prevent Siddhartha from developing a desire for renunciation and spiritual inquiry, he was never exposed to sickness, old age, death, or any form of suffering.. This is also a certain type of conditioning that Siddhartha had to undergo, where he did not get to experience life's realities.

As a young prince, Siddhartha lived a luxurious life far away from any kind of suffering, he had everything, the most expensive clothing, jewels, chariots to travel, the most beautiful palaces, the most beautiful women, and the luxury of every kind. It is important to note that he had everything one desired and had enjoyed everything one can desire. There seemed to be nothing more one could desire for. His father had devised a cage of paradise to secure his son's future.

Siddhartha was kept far away from every possible suffering. Siddhartha, at the age of twenty-nine, had a shocking revelation when he encountered suffering – old age, disease and death. The impact was significant. He was disturbed and suffered much emotionally. It was as if someone woke him up. He took to action; he wanted to find the cause of it all.

For any ordinary person, disease, old age and death are very common experience, it seems too absurd if someone would risk their life, their riches and kingdom for such small matters. This is another kind of conditioning where one is desensitized to matters of existential realities. Today, computer games, cartoons, and films often portray excessive violence, murder, and atrocities, leading to a growing desensitization to violence among children and youth. The *Bobo doll experiment* is a classic case of how children, subjected to witnessing violence are conditioned to mimic behavior. Violence presented to children as entertainment and fun in cartoons have a significant impact. The same is carried forward as adults, we enjoy action-oriented movies or horror movies.

> Siddhartha looked back at the palace and said – "There is no palace, it is all on fire. In there, death is approaching every moment."

We may have observed social media posts where someone has met with an accident and is seriously injured. Various videos from all angles of the scene go viral. In these videos, some people are seen busy recording, others walk past as though nothing has happened, and some are attempting to take selfies. Onlookers have gathered out of curiosity, while the ambulance is stuck in the traffic jam, unable to reach the scene. All of this occurs while someone lies on the road, fighting for their life. Mankind has become insensitive. Human relations have become shallow and at the most a matter of convenience.

Fortunately, Siddhartha was a sensitive man. He decided to leave home immediately to find a permanent solution to eradicate suffering. He probably found purpose in life which was otherwise missing, and life had become very monotonous. He must have experienced boredom for sure. In this moment of awakening, luxury no longer mattered to him. He could no longer be lured by beautiful women, music or dancing. He was finished with all of it – power, money, prestige, luxury and pleasure.

When Siddhartha was leaving his palace, his charioteer requested him to look back at his palace, his family, and friends and return to them. He said to Siddhartha that the path he was choosing is an arduous one, with a lot of difficulties which he has not been familiar with. Siddhartha looked back and said, "There is no palace, it is all on fire. In there, death is approaching every moment."

To have the eyes of Siddhartha, one needs to be capable enough to see the futility in power, prestige, money, luxury and pleasure. This requires much courage. In this quest, if you would go and donate all that you have to someone, you will only get more miserable. It is not about renouncing your wealth, or renouncing family or something else. You are not to force it on yourself. When you realize that the stones you are carrying are not real diamonds, you drop them immediately, you don't need intelligence, and you will not need much courage to throw them away either. It seems like common sense.

Taking such a decision to move to the forests for young Siddhartha was probably easy in this sense. He had no more worldly desires that would become an obstacle in his journey towards self-realization. Young Siddhartha had dropped his illusions.

He did not renounce the world, to gain something from the other world. The worldly desires had simply dropped. His renouncing the world was not an act, but a happening.

Although Siddhartha, was on the right path, he was not all right. His mind was still at play. This is what mind does, when you are not happy with what you are doing, it recommends you to go the other way, in the opposite direction in search of happiness. Siddhartha left the material only to choose the spiritual. He had taken meditation too seriously and to an extreme. Take note that one requires a strong sense of 'I' to take matters to great extremes. Without this sense of 'I', no penance is possible. Siddhartha had tortured his physical body for many years in sadhana. He was no doubt a man of peace, but he also observed great violence over himself by putting his body through much hardships.

Siddhartha spent six years in the forests of India, yet he had not found his answers. By the end of six years, he was fed up with his search which yielded no results. He sat under a bodhi tree in a pure state of let go; he was done with everything – he had no desires for the worldly or any aspirations for the spiritual. This is when he had the realization of balance. This is when he became aware, and walked the middle path. He became known as the Buddha – the awakened one.

Chapter Seventeen

The fist is deformed

"Let go the weight of seriousness;
Enjoy the playful rhythm of life."

The legendary laughing monks of China traveled from village to village. They were poor monks without much possession yet were full of joy. In every village they came by, they would laugh their hearts out, in turn, all the villagers would laugh. Laughter is contagious. The three laughing monks were loved by everyone. In this way, the monks spread joy all over China without saying a single word.

One day it happened, one of the monks died. The villagers wondered what would happen to the other two, they probably would be sad about the situation. The villagers found that the other two monks were laughing out loud. This was strange, so the villagers asked, "How can you be laughing when your friend has died?"

For the very first time, the two monks spoke. They said, "We are laughing because our friend has won. We would always wonder who would die first? and he has defeated us. We enjoyed each other's company all our life. There is no better way of saying goodbye to our beloved friend. We can only laugh."

The villagers helped the monks to prepare the body to be put on the funeral pyre. As the flames were lit, there were explosions and fireworks that they had never seen before. The monk who died had hidden firecrackers in the folds of his clothing before he died. He had surely beaten the other two friends. He had the last laugh.

> In Stillness, you become a witness to all that is. You are not in concentration or in contemplation. You accept everything as it is.

Life is nonserious, yet we approach it with great seriousness.

Children are filled with laughter, often laughing for no reason at all. However, as they grow older, their laughter subsides, and they find themselves laughing less and less. As they become busy pursuing studies and careers, and taking on important positions in society, their laughter further diminishes. They become increasingly concerned with 'what others might think,' making laughter feel less natural. When you cannot laugh freely, you have become uneasy. It appears that if you have to be taken seriously in today's world, you need to have a serious outlook.

It happened once, a great king, who had won many wars and also was known for his wisdom and sensibility was found drinking, cracking jokes, and enjoying in his court. A great scholar had come to visit him. Seeing the situation at the court and the behavior of the king, the scholar remarked, "Oh king, I did not expect this. I have heard that this court of yours is known for intellectual insights and wisdom. This court has insulted me, I am ashamed to be a witness to the behavior in the court. I am leaving the court immediately".

The King said, "Dear sir, please wait, allow me to reply to you, and then you can decide if you would like to leave. Please look at the bow in that corner. The strings of the bow are not tied to the bow. The bow is not ready to shoot an arrow. Bow is relaxed. If I always have the bow tied to a string, the bow remains in a state of stress at all times. This is not good for the bow as the bow will lose its elasticity. It will break down."

When you are always serious, it is sickness. Anything too much is a sickness. We often make mountains out of molehills. Patience is not even skin deep. Just a small thing, and we flare up, and are full of anger. Serious people cannot tolerate anything. They are too busy pursuing. You can also find such impatience with perfectionists. perfectionists are very serious people. They suffer much.

The great sages of the past were known for their meditation and wisdom. There are many stories in mythology that narrate their anger issues as well. When in meditation, even the smallest disturbance, they would be outraged and in anger would burn or put curses on those responsible for disturbing them. Such anger and outrage! How are they able to manage it? Wisdom and meditation would sober an individual with compassion and love, but it has been the other way around. Something does not add up.

In Stillness, you become a witness to all that is. You are not in concentration or in contemplation. You accept everything that is happening inside and outside you. You are in tune with existence. If someone disturbs you, you accept the disturbance as it comes. You respond to the situation instead of reacting in anger. A spiritual person lives non-seriously. Stillness has nothing to do with seriousness. You are at ease with yourself and everything around. You are in harmony.

A master once met a woman who was too serious about everything. He showed a tight fist to her and asked, "If I always keep my fist like this what would you call it?" She said, "It is deformed". He opened his palm fully and asked "What if I always had my palm open in this way?", She said, "This is another kind of deformity". The teacher said, "If you understand this much, you will lead a good life". In that moment, she was transformed.

In pursuit of the extraordinary, we miss the ordinary. Life is in the ordinariness of everything, just as they are. Nothing special. When you try to make things special, you become serious.

Chapter Eighteen

Pendulum

"Stillness - the point at which the pendulum of duality stops."

Life exists in duality. For the good to exist, bad is necessary. For the bad to exist, the good is necessary. Otherwise, where is something bad or good if there are no boundaries?

You see a mango up a tree. You may say the mango is outside. But as soon as you eat it, it enters your body, gets digested, and becomes a part of you. The mango is inside. What is outside becomes the inside.

Energies are exchanging, boundaries are merging and separating. Dualities are meeting and merging continuously.

What we experience as our life, is in between birth and death. When we are born, we eat plants, fruits, and vegetables. When we die, we become the soil and the soil nourishes the plants and trees. This is the circle of life.

When we breathe, we take in oxygen and release carbon dioxide, while the trees breathe in carbon dioxide and releases oxygen. As the Chinese Zen master Tozan says, "*Blue Mountain is the parent of the white cloud. White cloud is the child of the blue mountain. Both are independent yet dependent.*" In this way we can see that we are all one with everything, but two at the same time.

Our body and mind are not two but appear two. When you are experiencing stress, your physical health deteriorates. When your physical health deteriorates, so is your mental functioning. They are two sides of the same coin.

Based on your experiences, you may have an idea of what is good and what is bad. But is it really so? What is good for you may be bad for another, and what is bad for you may be good for another. A hero in one community is a villain for another. Duality in this sense, serves as a utilitarian function. Mind is continuously in movement between the dualities, like a pendulum. When you explore your mind, you will often cross paths with the judgements of good and bad and this further impairs your ability to understand various aspects of psychological realm.

So, is Ego good or bad?

The first and foremost function of the living organism is of survival. Life has self-organized and equipped itself from the point of survival. If there is no act of procreation, there would be no more life, all species would cease to exist. All traits and qualities that we have – desire, fear, anger, sadness, cunningness, lies, selfishness, lust, love, passion, ego, and just about every other quality has a role to play in one's survival. They are tools designed for survival. If life did not need them for its survival, then probably evolution would have eliminated it from its design. Even our acts of accumulation, of wealth, power prestige etc., are all many names and representations of ensuring our survival. Survival is the bottom line.

Your very being, is not your doing, it has come as a gift to you. Because of your past conditionings of good and bad, right and wrong, you are bound to have a one-sided view of everything. In your Stillness, you are not to engage in judging something. The opinionated debates of what is good and bad, right and wrong are endless and in the journey of self-discovery, you may find yourself lost, taking sides – for or against. Hence the emphasis on witnessing.

> Peace is not a goal or objective of Stillness. Peace is your inner reality when you drop the mind.

In practicing Stillness, you sensitize yourself with all the tools that life has made available. When you master the tools, you can master the Self. In the current situation, you have all the tools, but they are not well organized and you are unaware of the potential they carry. A knife can be used to cut vegetables and has potential to kill someone too. But if you do not know how to handle the knife, you are in trouble. You may end up injuring yourself and those around you. Knowledge is dangerous in the hands of those who are unaware.

One needs discipline and training to handle the tools. Stillness is your training ground. Being a witness in silence, elevates your quality of being. When you are no more judging from the standpoint of duality, you have risen above duality. This witnessing can bring a higher understanding of the Self. It is the mind that is always engaged in duality. Your consciousness is above the mind. What differentiates you from a mosquito or any other life form is your level of consciousness. When you rise in your level of consciousness, you become more human, otherwise there is not much difference between humans and other animals or insects. The fundamental nature is the same.

Mankind is capable of desiring, dreaming, and manifesting imagination. The mind actively pursues these "wants," pulling you in multiple directions. What you experience as stress is the result of this constant pushing and pulling that occurs within the mind. It is engaged in a lifelong pursuit. We often say, "*life is a roller coaster ride.*" However, this phrase suggests a false sense of centeredness, implying that life is a roller coaster. In reality, the mind can never be centered; it exists in constant movement between dualities, forever chasing after desires. It is in fact the mind, which is the roller coaster through which you experience life.

Eventually, when one grows weary of the relentless pursuit and feels overwhelmed by life's demands, one begins to seek peace and happiness. Even in this search, the mind tends to acquire knowledge and then turns happiness and peace into objectives to be pursued. Once again, it tries to make enlightenment and a place in heaven a goal, taking you on another ride in the spiritual realm. Ignorance enveloped in knowledge is not real knowing.

Peace is not a goal or objective of Stillness. Peace is your inner reality when you drop the mind. It can never be a goal that you can pursue.

Chapter Nineteen

Hope

"Throughout life, one can never be certain of
Living long enough to take another breath."

To desire, is to hope. Desire lives through hope. When you hope, you are postponing something. When you say you are hoping, then you have moved to an unknown future. You have postponed.

You hope that 'one day, when you have achieved all your dreams, you will relax'. But what about today? What about now? In hope of the tomorrow, you go on sacrificing today.

You may argue that hope is also a good thing. Yes, for someone who feels hopeless, hope can be a temporary relief. Already he is suffering much through hopelessness, maybe a little bit of hope can help him regain some energy to get through this day. Maybe in this way at least, he will suffer a bit less today. But this is a lie we tell ourselves, and in this way, live a life full of lies. Hope helps you to endure your suffering today, but you are not doing good today. It should be noted that hope cannot awaken you from suffering. If happiness is what you are hoping for, it cannot create happiness today. Suffering, has the potential to transform you, but not hope. Hope gives continuity to suffering because hope is from the future, not from the present. Due to hope, more time is invested in suffering. If the desire you are hoping for is not fulfilled, the extent of suffering will correspond to the emotional investment you have made with your hope. Some go on for decades in hope and suffer. So much time is lost in suffering.

> Suffering has the potential to transform you, but not hope. Hope gives continuity to suffering.

Hope must be transformed into action. When you are taking action, there is nothing to hope for.

Once a great samurai felt insulted and dishonored by his servant at home. The samurai challenged the servant to a duel to restore his honor. The servant knew he was in trouble. He knew that the samurai was capable of chopping his head off in one blow. So, the servant ran to a Zen master's house from the backdoor. He confessed to the master saying, "I am in trouble, and have come to take refuge."

The master said, "Come here and sit down. You have to fight the greatest samurai warrior. There is no doubt he is capable of taking your life in no time. But don't be worried. I will teach you to hold a sword. You just learn how to hold the sword and then you must hit him hard. It doesn't matter where just hit him hard with all your power". "You just be total; this is the only way for you to survive the fight" and he said "Don't be half-hearted when you hit him. Wherever you hit him, hit him with all your might and totally. And in doing so you will be a winner".

The poor servant could not believe what the Zen master was telling him. He said, "Master, I came to take refuge, but you are asking me to go back and face the challenge and get myself killed!!", The master said, "There is no point in hiding or running away, the samurai will anyway hunt you down". "No doubt the samurai has never lost in war, he knows all the techniques of the sword, but you must be total when you hit him and you just hit him anywhere you want spontaneously, and this is your only option"

The servant, for the first time in his life, mustered courage and learned how to hold the sword. He said to the master "I have no chancc to survive, but I will do as you say and I seem destined to die today anyways, but why not do it with all I have got, in totality"

The servant returned to the house and came in front of the great samurai. Holding the sword, he challenged the samurai and said loudly "Now come on"!

The samurai was surprised listening to the servant's roar. He thought maybe the servant took time as he was afraid and he has come to ask for forgiveness, but no, the servant is challenging him. He recognized the sword of the Zen master and asked "Where did you get this sword from?" The servant said, "From the same master who taught you the sword fight. But right now, I don't have time to discuss the sword, you come and fight with me. Let this be finished, It is either me or you today, but I guarantee you surely, not both will survive"

Hearing this and the servant's confidence, the samurai just for a moment, was a bit worried, and then he said to himself, "I have had years of training and have won several wars and I am the undefeated swordsman in the country, and this man is just a servant"

The fight began and the servant just went hitting the samurai wherever he could. The servant would manage to lift the sword high and suddenly hit hard on the samurai's toe. While the samurai would try to recover from a toe injury, servant would lift the sword from the ground and hit the samurai's nose and then he would swing the sword sideways and hit the samurai's knee. The samurai was at a loss, he knew how to fight with all trained warriors and swordsmen, he knew how to block a sword attack from a trained swordsman but he wasn't sure how to handle the servant as the servant was doing all kinds of crazy things and had gone rogue.

The samurai was unable to face the blows coming in from all over from the servant. The samurai finally had to accept defeat.

Hope is not a support system. The servant was not given any hope for the future. He was asked to face the situation, to be total and spontaneous. Here the servant just did whatever he could do at his best and had dropped any idea of winning. He lived totally in the fight and fought from moment to moment. For him, every moment was his last moment, he had no time to think about the future.

You have no control over the results. Have you given your best? That is all that matters.

It is prescribed to people to do good so that the resulting fruits will be good. For example, people do good deeds in the hope to cleanse themselves of past wrongdoings. Today it is all about how to do the least amount of work and maximize the fruits, or even better you do not have to work but you want all the fruits. For example, people outsource prayers and someone else will pray on their behalf in a place of worship. But have you observed those who complain that they did everything good, but they are not getting the desired results? Life is never unfair. The great intelligence is observing and recording all your actions. When you do something in the hope that good fruits will come by, you are in greed of good fruits. In greed, the act is never total. You are not fully invested in what you are doing.

Reflect on hope and be total in your Stillness.

Chapter Twenty

Collecting seashells

"Drop the words."

In the world of science, everything is very objective. Anything once discovered belongs to the whole world. It is available to you too.

In the world of spiritual, the discovery is very personal and an inner journey that everyone has to experience on their own. No one can lend it to you, not even a Buddha. My experience will always remain my own. This is one journey that asks for you to be truly authentic and original.

That is why Buddha says, '*experience cannot be borrowed.*' Today it is a world of information overload, and this is something we need to deal with on a day-to-day basis. In this process of research and exploration, you start collecting information. It gives the mind a sense of satisfaction, security, accomplishment, and understanding. The mind starts to believe.

We believe because we do not know. If you know something, you will never believe it. Belief ceases to exist. Belief 'is' when it is someone else's experience, not your own authentic experience. Do you believe that the taste of honey is sweet or do you know that the taste of honey is sweet? If you have never tasted honey and I would have told you that honey is sweet please believe me, would you ever know the taste of honey by keeping your belief in me? Such is the case with all beliefs. Words become empty without experience. What use is it, if we go on collecting such words and beliefs?

Just information will not help. You may become knowledgeable but it can never satisfy you, no matter how much information you go on collecting. The inner dissatisfaction is the very reason you go on collecting. You are compensating real experience by accumulation of knowledge. It is true in all aspects of life. The proof of the pudding is in the eating.

> Knowledge is an outside phenomenon, while wisdom is inner. Borrowed knowledge becomes a hindrance in your path of growth.

Words are but empty containers. They are meaningless when empty. When I say something, my experience is expressed in the form of words. When I say 'Honey is sweet', the words contain my experience of honey. In your journey, experience everything you come across firsthand. Your authentic experience will help you develop the roots necessary for your growth. This is what Buddha means, when he says, "*Do not believe in anything simply because you have heard it. Do not believe in anything simply because it is spoken and rumored by many. Do not believe in anything simply because it is found written in your books. Believe nothing, no matter where you read it or who said it, unless it agrees with your reason and common sense.*"

Wisdom rooted in you, from your own experience, brings transformation in life.

You can repeat words of borrowed wisdom, but it will not help. Never repeat what you have not experienced yourself. Such knowledge becomes a hindrance to your growth. This information and knowledge you go on collecting is borrowed from others. Wisdom grows within you from your own experience. Knowledge is an outside phenomenon, while wisdom is inner. Knowledge clings to the surface and gives you a sense of pride and accomplishment, but if you stick to it, it keeps you closed and farther away from experience and understanding. Understanding cannot be studied or taught. It comes from one's own experience.

In the process of self-discovery, to realize the truth, you need to be authentic. Being authentic is the foundation of your practice.

Chapter Twenty-One

Originality

"The mirror shines, when the dust is cleared"

You are unique. There is no one like you. But you are busy becoming someone else. In every field, there are star performers, but it is not necessary that one has to become like them. Take inspiration, but do not imitate and make a goal of becoming a replica of someone. Do not compare yourself with anyone.

Existence is unique, all life forms are unique, so why try to be a copy of someone else? A rose, if it thinks of becoming a Lotus or a marigold, then there are no more roses in the world. In reality, even two roses are not the same. They are unique. Existence does not repeat anything.

You have to discover your authentic being.

We often compare ourselves to others, seeking external validation and getting busy trying to emulate someone else because we are not taught to respect ourselves. When self-respect is not made explicit, we tend to take ourselves for granted. The problem arises when we are taught to respect others, but not ourselves. We are conditioned to sacrifice for others, where the needs of family, friends, and society always come first, leaving our own needs to be considered only to the end. This habit leads to a disconnection from ourselves.

Consequently, you may feel guilty for prioritizing your own needs ahead of others. Once the mind is conditioned this way, auto-suggestion takes over, and your mind begins to police your thoughts for conformance. Additionally, societal expectations push us to conform to ideals, implying that you are not worthy or respectable as you are, and that you must strive to attain some external standard of respectability. This constant comparison at every stage of life profoundly affects how you see yourself.

> You are unique, there is no one like you. Existence does not repeat anything.

The corrupted conditioning you have undergone does not allow you to respect others in a true sense. You tend to show respect only when someone becomes 'someone' – educated, wealthy, successful, or famous. This same respect is often withheld from those deemed ordinary. In this sense, respect becomes utilitarian. Consequently, you also fail to respect yourself genuinely. All these ideas of respectability stem from the ego, leading to a hierarchy where some are viewed as higher and others as lower. The mind is filled with divisions and discrimination, and it begins with you. Witness your mind's discriminations and contemplate on the importance of self-respect.

When you recognize your individuality, you gain the ability to see the uniqueness in everything that exists. The notions of superiority and inferiority, of higher and lower, simply drop away. The gestalt shifts. You will come to respect yourself and everything around you, feeling a sense of completeness within. This inner wholeness will prevent others from manipulating or dividing you. While others may still perceive you as a failure or an inadequate imitation of someone else, what truly matters is how you view yourself. Be original and true to who you are.

With individuality comes total freedom. All dependency dissolves, allowing you to stop pretending to be someone else, thus revealing your authentic Self.

Chapter Twenty-Two

Seagulls of happiness

"Contentment is your greatest wealth"

Happiness is something everyone looks forward to; everyone wants to be happy. The trouble is, many are unaware of where to actually find it. The mind often believes that happiness can be obtained through acquiring. This belief is a result of conditioning. Happiness is perceived through gains, whether material or emotional.

For example, a person who owns an ordinary digital watch and has an interest in watches may believe they would be much happier if they owned a highly expensive, diamond-studded watch. While both watches tell the same time, there is an association of happiness tied to the expensive item. This is the game of the mind, where the measure of happiness is reflected in the price tag. An ordinary digital watch and a diamond-studded watch both fulfill the same function – they tell time. If your primary concern is time, any watch will suffice. If your true concern is real happiness, then time does not matter, nor does the watch itself.

However, the mind is engaged in a serious pursuit of the expensive watch, rationalizing that this pursuit is worthwhile. Today, our pursuit of happiness is often quantified by money. If you equate happiness with a price tag, then happiness has lost its intrinsic value. In the world of business, 'Time is money.' In life, if time is measured solely in terms of money, you have lost the value of time itself.

You may think that once you possess the object of your desire and fulfill your dreams, you will be happy. But this line of thinking is a product of your conditioning.

Success is measured in terms of money. Love is measured through money. Sacrifice is measured through money. Money has become the currency of how you value life and this is where mankind has fallen. Life is immeasurable. Life is an experience. Love is something to be. Love is something to be felt, not measured.

> Happiness is right here and now. Life is happening to you every moment and happiness is inside you.

Happiness as a pursuit of gains is wrong understanding. The price you pay for pursuit of this kind of happiness is - lost time, failed relationships, stress, deteriorating health and suffering. In the end, you are looking for answers to "what is the meaning of life?". Only humans have this question, a flower does not bloom to ask the question, "what is the meaning of life?". When the flower blooms, it gives out its fragrance. It does not look for gaining something, it simply becomes an offering.

When you contribute to life, life amounts to something. When you contribute to happiness, happiness amounts to something. When you contribute to love, love amounts to something. With contribution comes value. However, this contribution should not be equated with a monetary price tag.

Only when you have something can you truly contribute. If you have experienced love, you can be loving. If you have known happiness, you can share happiness. This is rooted in your being; the true value lies in your essence, not in your possessions. The meaning resides in your being.

If you lack anything to contribute, you may only understand the language of taking, accumulation, and gaining. This reflects a desire to compensate for something you feel is missing – a sense of incompleteness that you wish to fulfill.

Happiness is right here and now. Life is unfolding around you every moment, and happiness resides within you. Yet, you have been preoccupied with pursuing it externally.

A boy was living by the seashore. He loved seagulls. Every day he would go to the beach to meet the seagulls and play with them. Whenever he went to the beach, the seagulls would come. His father who was a fisherman, got an idea. He said to his son to catch a few seagulls and bring it to him. The next day, the boy went to the beach, the seagulls hovered above him, but would not come down.

Life is a happening; you cannot force it in any way. The very effort to force life into something brings misery. You can only be receptive in anticipation. You cannot demand. For example, you want to sleep. You go to bed and simply wait. You are not to do anything. Just be in a state of rest and you slowly move into sleep. You cannot force sleep. If you want to relax, you simply stop engaging with whatever you are doing. Only then relaxation is a possibility. You cannot force relaxation to happen. So is the case with happiness, you cannot pursue happiness either.

Existence is not direct, like a bullet. It takes a very indirect route, it is circular. Life is not in a hurry. There is a saying, "*Nature does not hurry, yet everything is accomplished.*" There is no specific goal to be achieved. Just 'being' is its own goal. You just hang around likc thc fragrancc of a flower.

In your pursuit of happiness, you are constantly in the business of planning for the future. Planning and doing things in a way so that you can achieve the results as fast as possible. Speed keeps you restless; You are always in a state of tension.

The seagulls sensed the directness of the boy. He was in pursuit of catching hold of the seagulls and so they hovered over him but did not come down. When the boy had no motives, the seagulls came down to play with him. This is how it happens even with happiness. When you have nothing to do with happiness, suddenly it is there, you have it. Happiness was there all along, but you were the one who went missing. You had made it a far-away goal and were too busy pursuing it.

The seagulls of happiness are available to you when you are in a state of let go.

This is the secret to being happy. Just be available. If you always think of pursuing, your happiness is somewhere else, then it will never be where you are.

BEING A WITNESS

Chapter Twenty-Three

No work, No food

"Be Industrious.
Be active in spirit, but passive in expectations."

In ancient Hindu traditions the practice of seeking alms is part of renunciation and spiritual discipline. You can observe that Stillness is ingrained in such ancient practices such as receiving alms food. The meaning is significant. Bhiksha is not considered begging in the worldly sense, but a symbol of humility and detachment from material life. This act is intended to teach humility. The phrase, 'Bhavati bhiksham dehi', is used while asking for alms food. Bhavati – is a specific mode of addressing, Bhiksha – represents alms food. Dehi – requesting to give. Renunciates are traditionally expected to live by collecting food through alms, without hoarding or demanding. One must accept whatever is given without preference or complaint.

In the brahmin rituals, '*upanayana*' is one of the traditional samskaras or rites of passage that marks the acceptance of a student by a teacher or guru. As part of the ritual the student is introduced to this practice of asking for alms food by stating 'Bhavati bhiksham dehi'. This is a device designed to enable the student to be a witness to their ego. Ego is something so close, it is not easy to grasp it. A device is necessary to bring out our ego so that one can become aware of it. Asking for alms food in this way is significant as this simple device brings your awareness to the ego.

> 'Bhavati bhiksham dehi' is a device designed to bring your awareness to your ego.

I recall a story of Sri Adi Shankaracharya. He was a young boy. He went out in the neighborhood for Alms food. He knocked on one house, and said, "Bhavati bhiksham dehi."

The Lady of the house came out with a few berries in her hand and was weeping. He asked, "Why are you weeping mother?".

She said, "No, it is nothing, son".

Shankara insisted, "You are like a mother to me. Please tell me why do you weep?". She said, "I do not have much to offer, as my husband brings only a mere handful of food home. He says hoarding food is sin."

Shankara commented, "The wise who control past, present and future understand the universe as plainly as a berry seen in the palm of the hand."

He moved on to the neighboring house where he saw heap of grains, coconuts and other fruits put on display. The man of the house came up and said "take some alms" for which Shankara said "To hoard food is a sin. So, I will not touch your stock. Distribute your food supply to the poor and needy."

Those who have not understood the significance of 'giving' bhiksha approach it with greed in mind. Spiritual practices in unawareness deteriorates the values instilled in traditional practices. Be a witness of your own Self when you give or receive something. Observe your own tendencies in your practice of Stillness.

In recent years, there have been individuals entering monastic life for reasons other than genuine spiritual seeking, such as avoiding work or seeking economic support. Commercialization of meditation, pranayama, yoga and exploitation of followers is also a reality and a growing concern.

Hyakujo, the Chinese Chan master, at the age of eighty, would work with his students in the fields, attending to the gardens, preparing the ground, and tending to the trees.

The students were concerned to see the old teacher working hard. Hyakujo never listened to their advice to take rest. So, one day they hid his tools. That day, Hyakujo did not eat. The next day also he did not eat. The students got worried. They thought he is not eating as he is angry with them for hiding his tools.

The students put his tools back in its place the following day. Hyakujo worked that day and he ate food as before. In the evening, he instructed his students, "No work, No food."

Hyakujo's statement, is not merely about the value of labor; it is a radical teaching about presence, self-reliance, and spiritual responsibility. He is instructing his students that work is not separate from meditation. Whether it is sweeping the floor or cutting vegetables, the act is the practice. There is no sacred and secular divide. When Hyakujo works in the fields, he is fully present, embodying the same awareness and discipline as he would on a meditation cushion. By refusing to eat without working, he teaches that spiritual life is not passive. It is not about withdrawal from life's demands, but about meeting life completely. Non-attachment does not mean non-involvement. His age only strengthens the point that 'practice is lifelong'. There is never a moment when you retire from being fully awake.

Chapter Twenty-Four

There are no accidents

"In Stillness witness inaction in action and action in inaction."

It happened in the seventh century, the time when the renowned master Nansen lived in a self-made hut on Mount Nanquan in China. It had grown into a small monastery as students would come to study under him. The monastery was divided into the eastern and the western hall. There lived a beautiful cat in the monastery. The cat would sometimes be with the students of the eastern hall and sometimes with the students of the western hall.

One day it happened, when Nansen had gone out to the town, there was a huge fight about who owns the cat, very similar to how kids fight over a toy. It was evening and the fight had not settled. Nansen upon returning saw the fight and had to settle the matter.

Nansen held the cat and announced to the students "If you can say a word of truth, then the cat will be yours. Otherwise, I will have to put it to the sword so each of you can own one half." There was absolute silence in the hall. Everyone was wondering, what is the truth that can be said? What if they made a mistake in speaking something that is not true? In this dilemma, No one could answer Nansen.

Nansen cut the cat in two and said both groups could have the cat and the problem was solved. A little later that evening, Joshu, another student of Nansen returned from the market, Nansen told him of the incident. Joshu thereupon took off his sandal, put it on his head, and walked off. Nansen said, "If you had been there, the cat would have been saved!"

Whether this event really happened or not, what we should take away is that the expression of truth is in its spontaneity. If this expression is hindered by what is learnt then, it is not easy to be truthful.

Life is a series of causes and effects that we experience. We are affected by the consequences of our unconscious acts. Karma is born out of unconscious patterns, habits, and tendencies (Vasana). If the act is done consciously, we are not affected by the outcome.

When you are conscious, your thoughts and emotions cannot be manipulated by anyone. But when you are not conscious, you are not in control, you do not act but go on reacting to every situation. This is how karma accumulates.

When you act consciously, you are in the moment, total and spontaneous. The action is total and complete, there is no continuity. You do not accumulate any karma as there is no carrying forward. While an unconscious act has a continuity to it. We are reactive to the situation. Every reaction spawns another situation, and this continues.

Buddha was once passing through a village. A local villager started abusing Buddha with much anger. He was called names in public and asked to stop his teachings, calling him fake. Buddha stood there, calm and composed, listening to the man. Once the man stopped his abuses, Buddha spoke. Buddha said, "Tell me, if you brought a gift to someone and the other person did not receive the gift, then to whom does the gift belong to?" The man was surprised by Buddha's question. The man thought for a while and said, "It will belong to me as the other person did not receive it and I have paid for it". Buddha smiled back and said, "You are exactly right, now take back all that you have said and your anger, as I have not accepted it".

In Stillness our focus has to be on developing more awareness towards every aspect of the Self.

In awareness, life becomes an action, moment to moment. In unawareness, you are always in a state of reaction; like an accident waiting to happen.

We all are familiar with the words heaven and hell. They are often associated with Karma. Every culture has their own definition of how a heaven or a hell looks like.

In some heavens there are rivers of wine and alcohol, in others there are the most beautiful men and women. Similarly, hell is also described elaborately with the prescription of various punishments that one will be subject to if one has committed a crime in this world. Although these are imaginations of man, it will still be something of significance to contemplate on these imaginations. In the cold regions they describe hell to have freezing temperatures. In the warmer climatic regions, hell is described as very hot and punishments like one being fried in boiling oils are depicted.

In mountainous regions they are challenged by freezing temperatures and life is not easy. So, they imagine their hell to be such places with freezing temperatures. While we can see people from the plains go to the mountains for vacations and holidays to enjoy the cold temperatures. What seemingly is hell for someone is heaven for the other.

A great samurai, known for his valor, came to a teacher, and asked: "Is there a Heaven and a hell?". "May I know who is asking this question?" inquired the teacher. "I am a samurai" the warrior replied.

"You, a samurai!" exclaimed the teacher. "What kind of ruler would have you as his guard? Your face looks like that of a beggar." Hearing these words, the samurai became so angry that he began to draw his sword, and the teacher continued: "So you have a sword! Your weapon is probably much too dull to cut off my head." Samurai was even more angered by the insulting words.

As the samurai drew his sword in reaction to the master's words, the teacher remarked: "Here opens the gates of hell!"

At these words, the samurai, perceiving the master's discipline, sheathed his sword and bowed in respect.

In response, the teacher remarked, "Here opens the gates of heaven."

Heaven and hell are all your creation. If the samurai did not have the discipline of awareness, he being in anger, the situation could have turned to hell. He could have cut off the teacher's head. It is not just about the wisdom of the teacher to create a situation for the samurai to realize the answer to his question, but you can also to observe the readiness of the samurai, who had such a presence of mind and discipline, that in spite of being affected by anger, he was able to recognize the wisdom of the teacher.

Chapter Twenty-Five

The book is dead

"If you meet the Buddha on the road, kill him."

Shoichi was a one-eyed master. He taught his disciples in Tofuku temple. Day and night the entire temple stood in silence. There was no sound at all. Even the reciting of sutras was abolished by the teacher. His pupils had nothing to do but to sit still.

When the master passed away, an old neighbor heard the ringing of bells, and the recitation of sutras. The neighbor realized Shoichi was no more.

This happens when an authentic master is no more, the old habits come back. We are blinded by our conditioning. The years of conditioning are so strong and deep rooted, that breaking the mold of conditioning requires great courage and self-inquiry.

Books are just bundled paper without much value in the absence of a master. When there is no master, the book loses its spirit, the book is dead. A living master is capable of making the book come alive. Much is lost without the presence of an authentic master.

To understand truth, start with genuine curiosity. Doubt is good for an inquiring mind. It helps you to ask questions. Doubt allows you to be open. When you doubt, that means you are on the path of seeking and exploring. It paves the way to investigating the truth. Take cognizance that your doubt and curiosity is directed inwards.

> Doubt is a sign of intelligence.
>
> Belief is a hindrance in your path of self-discovery.

Only to say a Buddha, a Mahavira, a Shankaracharya, a Zarathustra, a Jesus or a Krishna have imparted the truth, you just believe in them, is simply not enough. Because this is what happens when you follow blindly: when the master is no more, the ringing of the bells and recitation of sutras. Where there is belief, there are no questions. While all the teachings have come from realized beings, you are yet to level up to them to understand what they may have said and meant. Where there are no questions, there is no self-discovery. The question too has to be authentic.

Some of the greatest minds in history have not rushed for answers, but have lived their questions. Questions have been their sacred flames. A Buddha asked '*why is there suffering?*' He left all comforts and sat under a tree with this question. Enlightenment came not from knowledge, but from deep, lived inquiry. Socrates asked '*what is virtue? What is truth?*' He questioned everything and everyone including himself. Isaac Newton asked '*why does the apple fall?*' He didn't just say 'gravity' and move on, he stayed with the question. Ramana Maharshi asked '*Who am I?*' Rene Descartes asked '*What can I know for certain?*' Doubt was his guide. Jiddu Krishnamurti asked '*Can the mind be free of conditioning?*' He challenged authority, systems, even spiritual traditions, staying with deep questions about freedom, thought, and awareness without rushing to easy answers.

Doubt is a sign of intelligence. Everyone is born intelligent. Belief is a hindrance in your path of self-discovery. That is why the expression, '*If you find the Buddha, kill him*' by Linji Yixuan. Here Linji is referring to Buddha as – 'knowledge from the outside'. In today's world of information flooding, knowledge from the outside is just unavoidable. Here is where one needs to observe caution. Linji is asking to rely on your doubt, because as you accumulate knowledge, you are moving farther away from your Self. All knowledge from the outside gives you the illusion of knowing without knowing anything at all. Doubt is the key to dismantling your conditioning, further leading you to your own clarity. When you walk through doubt, you will not find answers, but you will find your Self, which is the only truth worth knowing.

Chapter Twenty-Six

Pure water

"If your heart is pure,
all things in the world are pure."

Travelling in to nature, the forests, the mountains, the waterfalls, and the rivers fill you with great joy. Nature is beautiful. When you look closely, the beauty of nature is in its imperfections. You are appreciating the coming together of all imperfections. When it comes to your own life, you are continuously pursuing perfection. Anything that does not fall into your idea of perfection, you reject it, you are disappointed, you dislike it. You look for the perfect life, the perfect job, the perfect looks, the perfect partner, and the perfect house. Everything that matters to your life should be perfect. If it is not, you end up pursuing it to your idea of perfection, and in this pursuit, you invite suffering. The obsession for perfection moves you away from enjoying the moment. If something does not go your way, you may become very hard on your yourself and on those around you.

When you look at nature, everything is imperfectly arranged. You may say it is perfectly imperfect. But life is not happening the way you imagined it to be. You are conditioned about what is perfect. You have a certain fixed idea about it. If everything is so well arranged, and well planned, life becomes static, monotonous, boring. Such fixations bring misery. Everything in life is dynamic and spontaneous.

> Nature is perfectly imperfect.

When water is impure, it provides the necessary nourishment for the fish to grow. It is food for the fish. A fish cannot live in pure water. Pure water is dangerous for the fish. In this way impurity sustains life. So are life situations and the various conditionings for you. Life can be experienced as misery by carrying fixed ideas, or you can grow with the experiences that life offers.

Development of the Self cannot happen in a cultural void. Culture and traditions have an important and significant role in your conditioning and in shaping you into who you are today. You have had various experiences while going through the process of conditioning. It gives you a certain richness that is required for development. There is a possibility for your growth and transformation. What matters is whether are you available to life situations in awareness. When you become a witness to your conditionings, you become free from its grip.

A lotus plant always grows in muddy waters. Muddy waters represent the environment of conditioning and all that life is throwing at you. Growing in muddy waters represents the ability to unlearn in the process of discovering the Self. The Lotus flower floats on water, symbolizing balance and awareness. It symbolizes the ability to be in the world, but still not be consumed by it. It represents acceptance and is a symbol of spirituality.

Chapter Twenty-Seven

Secret key

"A door without a lock remains open. There is no key."

Our attention to thoughts, is nourishment to the thoughts. Attention is food. If you do not give any attention to your thoughts, the thoughts disappear on their own accord. In our practice of Stillness, the only way not to be distracted, is to observe your thoughts and let them flow. The thoughts may be good or bad, but let them be, and avoid any attention or engagement.

When you make an effort to avoid the thoughts, that is where you fall. The very effort will have the thoughts bounce back. Our attitude is not to avoid or engage, but accept the thoughts as they are. You cannot throw out any thoughts from your mind. It is impossible. The more you try, the more thoughts flow.

I have heard of a Tibetan story, A young man, was in search of an old monk who was known to have many secrets. The monk would not speak much. The young man was determined to get the monk to share his secrets. He said to himself, that he would devote himself in the service of the monk, so he may please the monk and get the secrets.

> When practicing Stillness, be a witness to your thoughts and do not feed them.

So, he stayed with the old monk, serving him day and night. The old monk said, "Young man, you are unnecessarily wasting your time. I am just a poor old man, I don't have anything to say, so I remain silent."

But the man persuaded, "Please give me the secret which opens the door of all the mysteries."

The winter was coming, and the monk did not want the young man to suffer the cold in his small hut. The monk knew it would be too hard on the young man. But any insistence to leave him was futile. The Young man continued to serve him day and night.

Finally, the old monk said to the man, "Today I am going to tell you the secret."

In Tibet, there is a mantra that religious people chant. He gave the mantra and said, "Everything is hidden in this mantra."

The young man said, "Don't try to fool me! I know this mantra, this is no secret. It is the most widely known mantra to all."

He said, "Yes, it is widely known. But the key is not known to all for opening it."

The young man was all excited to get the key.

The monk continued "The key is, while you are repeating the mantra, just for five minutes, don't let any monkey pop into your head."

The man said, "This is strange, I have chanted the mantra all along and monkey never appeared, What kind of a key is this?"

The Monk said, "Now, I have given the secret key to you, you may leave".

The Man packed himself and started walking down the hill from the hut. But strangely, even though he was not reciting the mantra, monkeys started appearing. He closed his eyes, and they were there. He started running, but the monkeys followed him. And slowly the monkey crowd was becoming bigger in his head.

He said to himself, "Why did I ask for a key? this is too much, how do I get rid of the monkeys? I am finished! I have not even started reciting the mantra."

He thought of an idea, he said, "Let me take a good bath in the cold river, maybe that will help in getting rid of the monkeys" But the more he tried to avoid them, the more monkeys popped up.

Then he thought, let me sit in meditation and burn some incense sticks, maybe that will help. But no, all he could think of in his meditation was monkeys and more monkeys. He tried the entire night without sleeping, but nothing worked.

By the morning, he was tired, and in anger, he shouted, "This old monk! he has tricked me, I need these monkeys out of my head!!". The man's only goal was to get rid of the monkeys. He got ready and rushed up the hill to the old monk and said, "I cannot handle this, please take away your key. The monkeys are driving me crazy"

The old monk replied, "That is why I was hesitant to tell anyone because the key is very difficult. Now you know why I remain silent"

The man said, "I don't want any key from you, Help me get rid of the monkeys. Please take the key back"

The monk said, "But, I have given it to you already, there is no way I can take it back. But you can do one thing. Never repeat the mantra and the monkeys will not follow you."

The man dropped the mantra, he dropped the key. On his way back down the hill, he realized there were no monkeys following him. He looked around again and there were no monkeys. He thought this was strange, and just to test the monk's words, he started to chant again and as soon as he started, there it was the monkey.

This story is not about the mantra or a secret code, but about our fragility of our mind. It is about how we form associations of unrelated matters and suffer the consequences of such associations. Our blind beliefs are many such associations that have deep rooted in us and results in mind suffering. Monkeys represent our continuous stream of thoughts. In your practice of Stillness, be a witness to your thoughts and do not feed them.

Chapter Twenty-Eight

Be total

"Be total, burn yourself completely."

It was early in the morning, a student was unable to sit quietly during the Stillness session, and Master found him murmuring something to himself while sitting. Master walked up to him and asked, "what happened?" The student replied that he was unable to sit Still as he had to rush to his office due to some urgent work.

The mind is in constant motion. Moving between, thinking about what has happened – the past, and what is about to come – the future. The mind is full of thoughts. You get engaged and preoccupied with the continuous feed of thoughts. Mind is never here, always there, somewhere. The practice of Stillness cannot be rushed. You have to be total in your practice only then you can apply it in life.

Live totally. You may have experienced a glimpse of this totality at some point in your life. When you love your work or are engaged in a favorite activity, you become engrossed in the moment. Even if someone speaks to you, you might not hear them. You may not even feel hungry and may skip your meals. Time ceases to exist. You enter a state of flow. Only when you finally complete the work you were so engrossed in, you suddenly realize how much time has passed.

Time moves differently when you are fully engaged. When you are feeling happy or immersed in your favorite activity, time seems to fly by. If you enjoy a movie, or a book or a game of chess or anything where you get fully involved, once you come out of the activity, you realize much time passed in what felt like moments. This realization of time happens only after the event itself. While you are happy, working on a project, or enjoying a movie, you are not concerned with time; you are living intensely in each moment.

Conversely, when you are experiencing sadness, time appears to move slowly. In moments of sadness, your mind oscillates between what has happened and what should have happened. As a result, time is stretched as we shift from the past to the future. You become anchored in the past when you are sad. But your mind is also racing towards the future state of happiness that it wants to be in, but is unable to. The speed at which we want to experience a future state defines our suffering. The more we are desperate to experience a future state while being anchored in the past, the more time feels like eternity.

Suffering need not be perceived only as a consequence of a significant disaster in life. It can also manifest in simple experiences, such as waiting for a bus or someone who said they would arrive at a certain time but has not yet. You may find yourself continuously checking your wrist watch, feeling as if time has slowed. When you are waiting for the bus or someone's arrival, every minute can feel like an hour. This intense anticipation for a desired state that has yet to materialize can be said as one is suffering – Time.

> When your are happy, time moves fast. When you are sad, time moves slow. In Stillness, time disappears.

Even in your dream, you experience something similar. The duration of the dream may be short but the intensity with which you experience and live a dream, is high. One may have experienced an entire life time within a single dream. This intensity makes your dream feel real.

In all the three states of happiness, sadness and dream there is one thing in common that time can expand, contract and also disappear for some time. The intensity with which you lived gave you a different experience of time. When you were happy and lived intensely engaged in your favorite activity, time in fact did not exist. Only when you came out of that state is when you realized that time has passed by quickly. When you were sad, you remained intensely waiting for the future which gave you an experience of time, but you ended up suffering however small the time period.

When dreaming, the intensity made the dream real, and you were unaware that you are actually dreaming. If the dream was good, you would not complain, but if you had a bad dream, you end up with much suffering. All of these can be said as a dream state as you are not conscious of your state of being.

As in your practice of Stillness, when you are conscious of your presence at all times both physically, mentally, outwardly and inwardly, you are in the state of 'Now'. In living this way, Time has no relevance and ceases completely. In your totality, time disappears. Bring this intensity and alertness, in your everyday life.

Chapter Twenty-Nine

Wonder

"The old pond
A frog jumps in—
The sound of water"
~Matsuo Basho

A haiku is a traditional form of Japanese poetry that consists of seventeen syllables. It is known for its simplicity and represents an act of Stillness. Haikus often capture a moment or scene in nature, conveying a sense of serenity, beauty, or a fleeting moment in a concise and evocative manner.

Here Basho's haiku needs to be visualized. Here is an old pond, tranquil and silent. A frog jumps in, and breaks this tranquility and silence. "plop" the sound of the water is heard.

One moment, there was no sound, and the next moment, we hear the sound of water. Where did the sound come from? After the sound was heard, where did the sound go?

It might sound funny to think this way in today's world as everyone knows that sound is produced due to vibrations. One can get very technical about it. This is knowledge interfering with a state of wonder. If you never knew about vibrations or waves, you would have probably stayed with the question. And if you would have stayed with the question long enough, your curiosity would have led you to 'somewhere'. This somewhere is authentic because it has come from you. An apple fell off a tree. Would you care? While there was one person who did! Isaac Newton wondered why the apple fell straight to the ground instead of moving sideways or upwards, further leading him to formulate the law of universal gravitation. The story of Archimedes reveals a simple truth about how discovery happens – not by force, but through flow. You don't force answers, but just soak in them and the answers will find you. When you stay in wonder long enough, there is every possibility that you may stumble upon your eureka moment.

It is interesting to observe that a joke said twice is no more a joke. The first time you burst into laughter because you experienced absurdity, but the second time heard the same joke, there is no more laughter in you as you now already know the punch line. Laughter is only possible if there is absurdity. Knowledgeability makes us lose the innocence, the state of wonder.

Similar to Basho's Pond, has it occurred that in our mind, where do these thoughts come and where do they go? You experience thoughts all the time, but have you paused to look at where exactly the thoughts arise from? This is the 'now' moment, to look at the creation of thoughts and go into the vast nothing from where the birth takes place.

Everything comes from nothing and goes back into the great nothing. Life is dynamic, life is never old; each and every moment, life is happening. It is forever fresh. Like an autumn tree that sheds its leaves and becomes green again or a river flowing. The rate at which change is occurring could seem to be slow or fast, but life is, at all times, creating, transforming, and refreshing itself.

Wonder is the feeling of amazement and curiosity about the world around us. Wonder often arises from encountering something new, unexpected, or beautiful. This sense of wonder is a powerful catalyst for creativity. When you encounter something that makes you wonder, it can spark your imagination and lead to creative thinking. Many creative works, such as art, literature, and scientific discoveries, have been born from a deep sense of wonder. When you wonder about something, you may feel compelled to explore it further, to ask questions, and to seek answers. Curiosity is a driving force behind creativity because it motivates you to investigate, experiment, and learn. Imagination is a fundamental component of creativity. Children often exhibit a strong sense of wonder, and this is expressed in their uninhibited creativity. They are full of questions. Give them a toy and the child is curious to know what it is made up of and may try to open the toy to see

> Life is dynamic. Life is never old. Each and every moment, Life is happening. It is forever fresh.

what's inside. But more often than not, they are shunned to not ask questions, not to break open toys and not to do the many things they end up doing. They are limited or restricted to explore their world in their own unique ways. This interferes with their independent thinking, curiosity, creativity and imagination. As children grow older with rote learning of readymade answers and are put on a track of education to accumulate more and more knowledge, they lose this childlike wonder.

Inspect on your own conditioning and knowledgeability, and how it may have affected your passion, curiosity and freedom of independent thought. While a large portion of the world are blindly anchored to discoveries made by select few, we often fail to acknowledge that existential questions are by large, something personal, and has to do with our own authentic experience.

Don't take anything that is in this book for answers, as this will hinder your growth. Let the perspectives help you think on the various dimensions of the Self, but let them not be answers. Let them not stop you from asking more questions. If you arrive at the same conclusions, that is a different matter. Even then, you own those answers and hence it is significant. In your life, you are the one to give birth to your own answers. The answers need to be authentic with your signature on it. This is your individual journey and it has to have your unique signature. When I say it has to be your own, It is not a matter of ego, it is a matter of authenticity. This is what gives your life – meaning.

Chapter Thirty

Worthiness

"You are enough."

An old master, revered by many, refused to initiate anyone as his disciple. All his life, kings, rich people and ascetics, asked him to initiate them as his disciple. He went on refusing. He always said, "Until I find a man who is deserving, who is worthy, I will not initiate."

The master was getting old, he was almost a hundred years old. Along with him grew up a boy. He would cook food, wash clothes and would get vegetables from the market. The boy himself now was a grown-up man. He had seen the master's denial all his life.

Everyone loved the master, but were tired and frustrated. They could not understand why the master would not initiate and why he is so stubborn.

But one morning the old man woke up. He came to his helper and said to him, "Run down the village and tell everyone that whoever wants to be initiated should come to me as soon as possible. Because by evening as the sun is going to set, I am going to die. I will be no more".

The young man said, "What are you saying!! and what about worthiness? I will not be able to know who is worthy in the village. Whom can I bring back?"

> When we acknowledge our own weaknesses and flaws, we realize that everyone is worthy.

The old master said, "Do not worry. It was only a device, because I myself was not ready to initiate anyone. It was against my dignity, so I chose to reject people as I doubted my own worthiness by saying, 'Unless someone is worthy and deserving, I am not going to initiate.' Now I am worthy, but the time too short. It is only today, in the morning, at sun rise, my own consciousness has risen to the ultimate peak. I am now ready. It does not matter who is worthy and who is not. What matters is that I am worthy. Just go and bring anybody! Go announce to the entire village that today is the last day of my life, and anyone who wants to be initiated should come quickly. Go and bring as many people as possible. There is no time to waste."

The young man was at a loss. There was no time to discuss the matter. He quickly ran down the hill as fast as he could. He reached the village marketplace and he shouted loudly, "Master is ready now, anyone who wants to become his disciple, hurry up and meet him."

The villagers could not believe him. Many didn't take interest in his announcement. While there were few, who out of curiosity said, "Let us go and see what is going on. This old man had refused all his life, and now suddenly he seems to have changed."

All kinds of people started toward the old man's hut. The young man was a little embarrassed as to the kind of people he was guiding along. One was a criminal who had just come out of jail, one's wife is dead, another was a drunkard, another had gone bankrupt due to gambling and the other few just out of curiosity as they had no work to do.

The young man was thinking, "How will I present these strange set of people to this old master who once had refused great kings, ascetics, and those who had come with earnestness to get initiated? And now master is going to initiate this strange gang!?"

They reached the hut, and the young man entered the hut and asked his master, "Should I call them in? I have managed to get fifteen of them."

The old man said, "Call them in quickly, it is already noon. You were gone so long, still you managed only fifteen?"

Young man said, "What can I do? Today is not a holiday. Everyone are busy at their work. I could only get this lot, but I must say all of them are absolutely useless, even I wouldn't initiate them. But upon your insistence I have got them."

The old man said, "No problem. Just let them come in." The master initiated all of them. They asked the master, "You seem strange, all your life you have insisted on worthiness. What happened to your principles? We all know we are not worthy; we just came here out of curiosity."

The old man laughed and said, "There was no principle, it was only to hide my own unworthiness. I was not yet a master. And I could not cheat anyone, I could not deceive those who came in earnestness. I took shelter behind this judgment that unless someone is worthy, I will not initiate them."

Everyone has their weaknesses and their own flaws. Everyone has done things they never wanted to do. Everyone has gone astray. No one can say that one is absolutely pure, and that they have no short comings. So, when the old man insisted on worthiness as a criterion, nobody argued with him.

On that day, the old master said to those fifteen disciples, "I bless you; you are now initiated. It does not matter if you are worthy or not. For the first time, I am worthy and if I am really so worthy, my presence shall purify your sins. My worthiness as a master will make you a worthy disciple. For all these years, I was depending on your worthiness and now I am no more dependent. My worthiness will do."

It was evening, the Sun is setting. As the master had announced, at sun set, he was no more.

Worthiness is not about living up to some standard that the world has set for you. It is not something you have to earn and only then you can prove your worthiness. It is not about how many achievements you can collect or how others see you.

Worthiness is something that is already within you, simply because you exist. You are born worthy. The universe, in all its vastness, created you with a unique essence, and that makes you inherently valuable. You do not need to prove anything to anyone, and you certainly do not need to seek validation from others to feel worthy.

Worthiness is not something outside of you. It is not about what you have or what you do; it is about being who you truly are. When you truly accept yourself – your strengths and your weaknesses – you are worthy, just as you are, this very moment. Stop looking outside for confirmation of your worth. Stop seeking approval from others. The moment you stop striving to be something you are not, and simply embrace who you are, you will realize that you have always been worthy.

It is about self-acceptance. When you live fully in the present, without any need to prove yourself, you naturally feel the freedom to express your true self. And in that moment, you will know that you are enough, just as you are.

GAINING CLARITY

Chapter Thirty-One

In search of a master

"When the student is ready,
The teacher will appear.
When the student is truly ready,
The teacher will disappear."

A young man was looking to find the right master for him. He read many books, visited many masters, and practiced under them. But each time, he was not sure if he had met the right master, so he would move to a newer place, and study under a different master. He had a certain idea of who was the right master for him. He was trying to fit the masters he met into his idea of the perfect master and to see if there was a match. In the process thirty years passed by, and he could not find the master.

How can you find a master? One needs eyes to be able to recognize something of value. If you want to be able to recognize an opportunity, you need a certain level of preparedness, otherwise, opportunities will pass by and you will not be ready. The meeting is possible when you are receptive. In being receptive you are. Otherwise, all your life, you can invest in knowledge and never find the truth.

> When the student is ready, the master appears. When the student is really ready, the master disappears.

Man is comfortable with lies. With truth he is uncomfortable. That is why the saying, '*truth is bitter*'. Truth in itself is not bitter. Similarly, your idea of a right master is a lie you tell yourself. It is your ego that is looking for the right master. If you ever encounter the right master, he will destroy your ego. That is the work of a master. The ego depends on lies, that which is false. Ego is continuously in a search for that which supports its existence. When you find someone who supports your idea, immediately you will appreciate him, as he is in support of your ego. The ego feels strengthened. You are looking for the one who will approve of you and your thoughts. This is how you go on missing the truth. You are not looking for truth, but something, or someone who can support your standpoint, your ego. This is the game of the ego. Then you move from one book to another, one master to another, constantly in judgment. You drift further away from realizing that which is.

A student has to sacrifice his ego and surrender to a master to know something of the truth. The sacrifice has to be total. In this totality, you find the master. The real question is not about the master, but about being a real student.

Once a theist asked Buddha, 'Is there God?' and Buddha responded, 'No, there is no God'. Yet another time, an atheist asked the same question and Buddha said, "Yes there is god". Another time, when the same question was asked by another person, Buddha remained silent. Observing Buddha and his responses to different people, his disciples were confused with the answers and wanted to know what is the real truth.

Buddha said, "I was answering the person who asked the question. The questioner, the time, and the situation were all different. The question is never the same. I had to shake them out of their ignorance." And he continued. "I was silent on one context because the question came from an innocent man".

Paramahamsa Ramakrishna was a great yogi of the nineteenth century. He was an ardent devotee of mother goddess Kali. One of the spiritual masters of Ramakrishna was Avdooth Totapuri. Totapuri was the reason Ramakrishna came to his ultimate realization.

One day, during Ramakrishna's practice of meditation, Totapuri said to him, "Look Ramakrishna, you have not progressed even a bit on the path of meditation. I am getting very impatient and I am leaving". Ramakrishna said, "Dear Gurudev, what can I do? Whenever I meditate, the figure of Mother Kali appears before my eyes."

Totapuri said "Then take the sword and cut her into two".

Ramakrishna was shocked upon hearing his master's advice. He loved Mother Goddess so much that he could not conceive of such an act. But he was a disciple, and he continued to enquire, "From where will I bring my sword from?"

Totapuri said, "Where did you bring the figure of Kali in your mind? Bring the sword from the same place". Ramakrishna said "All right, I will try"

Totapuri continued in his commanding voice, "Do it now! raise the sword, do not fear or panic, don't be afraid"

Ramakrishna immersed himself in meditation and, mother Goddess appeared. He was filled with tears. But as instructed by his master, Ramakrishna raised the sword and cut Kali into two. Suddenly the doors of freedom had opened as he immersed himself into samadhi.

The saying, '*when a student is ready, the master appears*', means, when the student is ready, the student is no more, he becomes the master. This is the death of the student and birth of a master. This is when rebirth happens. This is metamorphosis of a student into a master. Interestingly, when the student is truly ready, the master disappears. He transcends both.

Chapter Thirty-Two

Marrow

"Silence holds the answers that words can never express."

A story from mythology or fables can be enjoyed as entertainment or it can be applied for spiritual development. It depends on how one consumes the story. Our mind is interested in the entertainment, while it is not interested in spiritual development. The very idea of spiritual development is boring for the mind as it is against mind. It engages when it is about logic, beauty, magic, intellectual debates, but as soon as the subject of awareness is presented, the mind is not interested. The mind becomes very afraid. It tries to rationalize with you. It wants you to follow its way, and it puts forth its best to make you agree with it, because that is the only way it can survive.

Spiritual development is all about annihilating the Mind. Mind knows this fact very well. Mythological stories were not created solely for entertainment. It was a device designed to uplift mankind into liberation, freedom. In order to awaken we need to encounter the mind first. When you listen to a story, or a song, mind entertains itself with the words and makes you settle with the entertainment.

Kashmir folk tales for example, has a collection of twenty-five stories about king Vikramaditya and a betaal. Betaal means ghost. The king was assigned a task to go alone and fetch a corpse hanging on the branches of a very old tree in the cremation grounds. Vikramaditya was a brave man. He went alone to the crematory as asked. He spotted the old tree and saw the corpse hanging. As he decided to go up the tree to fetch it, the betaal in the corpse said "Hi!". Vikramaditya did not expect this. Meeting a dead corpse hanging on the tree branch is enough to scare the hell out of any person, but this corpse was speaking! The brave king expressed why he had come there. The betaal agreed to go with him but based on one condition. The condition is that Vikramaditya is supposed to maintain silence when carrying the betaal on his shoulders. If he breaks the promise, the betaal would come back to the tree. Vikramaditya agreed.

He got the betaal off the tree, put him on his back and started to walk. The betaal put another condition. This time betaal said, "the journey is very long, let me tell you a story and in the end, I will ask you a question. If you answer the question correctly, then I will be with you otherwise I will have to kill you and comeback to the tree." Vikramaditya agreed.

> Do not cling to words as words cannot express the whole truth.

On the way, betaal started describing a story. Vikramaditya got engrossed in the story being described. When they were very near to their destination, the moment came when the betaal finished the story and asked Vikramaditya a question about the story. Vikramaditya thought about the question. He answered the question honestly, because the betaal had put the condition that if he would not answer then the betaal with the right answer, the betaal would kill him and go back to the tree. The betaal listening to his answer said, "You have spoken. Now you have broken your promise of remaining silent." I am going back to the tree and flies away to the tree. Vikramaditya would again go back in search of the betaal and start all over again.

This story relates to our mind. Our mind has many tricks up its sleeve to engage us. It does not allow us to stay centered in awareness. It engages us in words and dialogues. It rationalizes and reasons on ideals and morals and keeps us busy.

Language is a medium of expression. It has a certain utility, but it also comes with limitations. It cannot define that which is inexpressible. Lao tzu says, '*The Tao that can be told, is not the eternal Tao*'. This is how he begins the verse of Tao te ching. Tao means – the way. He declared it upfront, in the very first line, that, this is a limitation of language. He declares it so that the reader is absolutely clear that anything that is said is not complete in its expression and may be bound to be misunderstood. This is a warning to the seeker that one should not just cling to words as words cannot express the whole truth. This is the reason we find the expressions like 'In search of truth' or 'discover the truth'. Truth cannot be handed over and is always a discovery and is always personal; hence, has to be experienced firsthand.

As soon as the truth is expressed in words it becomes false. Words falsify the whole truth. This is the paradox. Hence truth can never be expressed through words. That is why it is said, '*language of words is that from the ignorant*'. Words are merely a means, serving a purpose. In reciting a mantra, listening to a mythological story, or singing a devotional song, you may become curious and seek the deeper meaning within. There is hope that these mantras, stories, and songs will bring awareness – if you pay attention to what they are pointing to.

'Aham Brahmasmi', is one of the mahavakya (great saying) from the Upanishads. It means 'I am divine'. This is not a mere statement; it is pointing to something deeper. It is pointing to your original nature – your divinity. Ordinarily, the mind associates the word 'I' with the Divine, taking words literally in a self-centered way. Mind will start imagining about the divine. It gives an illusion that one is divine. Reciting or understanding a mantra in this way can only inflate ego. We need to acknowledge that such complete statements as 'Aham bramhasmi' were the result of discoveries from those who were self-realized. But if we take this and start repeating 'Aham bramhasmi' all is lost. Neither are we aware of Aham and nor the Bramha. Logic and intellect cannot solve something existential.

Logic has a limit. Beyond a certain limit all logic sounds absurd and meaningless. You can only get so far with logic.

But as we are in our own laboratory of the Self, investigating, let us look at the phrase linguistically. 'I' refers to the Self here. When you say 'I am divine', if 'you' the 'I' is the 'divine', then the word 'I' need not exist in the phrase, only the word 'divine' is enough. Why add two words to mean the same? It is linguistically incorrect expression of the truth. 'I' is unnecessary, but this is the challenge – how do you express the phrase 'I am Divine' without 'I'? The phrase will simply go out of context.

Let us suppose we rephrase it to remove the 'I'. We could say, "Divine is the only one that is". This is also not the whole truth. Then if something 'is', it also means that there is something that 'is not'. We can say for example, dinosaurs were there someday, today they aren't; Mankind is there today and one day it may not! If you drop the I and divine, only am-ness remains. The phrasc transcends duality. When you transcend duality, only silence remains. Observe the phrase in silence. The phrase can only be expressed through silence, in Stillness.

The phrase 'Aham Brahmasmi' or 'I am Divine' is indicating that if one can go beyond the current boundary of 'I' and expand the 'I' to encompass the whole universe, then 'I' loses its relevance and becomes one with the whole. This oneness is expressed through the word Divine.

While all this time 'I' was a problem in self-discovery, but now we want 'I' to be expanded and that too to the whole universe! This is a matter of scope. The ego as we discussed is the small 'I'. Its scope is limited. You are identified with yourself and marking your separation from the universe. When you expand the scope, everything becomes yourself, and then there is no 'other'. All becomes part of the whole.

You may consider your boundary of the physical for example to be your skin, the outer most layer. But is this your real boundary? If your skin is injured, you experience pain. Hence you may conclude that so long as we experience the physical, that is our boundary. Now the whole skin also is interacting with the outside air. Skin is breathing. We cannot survive without the medium of air. Any fluctuation in air, impacts our body as well, so we can see that we are connected. Similarly, the atmosphere is affected by the stars, planets and sun. Imagine if there is no sunlight, then there is no us. We can see the expanse of the 'I'. Ordinarily, we define boundaries, but we need to train ourselves to observe with more inclusivity.

'Tat Tvam Asi' is another mahavakya from the Upanishads translated as 'That Thou Art' or 'You Are That.' This phrase also conveys the idea that the individual self is identical with the universal, absolute reality.

On another note, Bodhidharma inferred, the journey of understanding is like the layers of the human body. At first, we only perceive the skin, which represents superficial knowledge. Beneath the skin lies the flesh, which symbolizes a deeper level of understanding. As we go still deeper, we reach the bones, our foundational structure. However, the true essence lies within the marrow.

Words are linguistically dual in nature. Every word has an opposite. Masters have been challenged for years, on how to express silence through words. The ultimate truth can only be expressed and experienced in Stillness.

We are in movement from ignorance to knowledge. As we gain knowledge, we realize there is something more and we move into ignorance. And once again the movement towards knowledge. We engage ourselves continuously in this duality. On the one side we have knowledge (words) and language (sound). On the other, there are no words and no sound. This is the duality. There is a third dimension which is the movement into witnessing and that of silence. This is where Stillness happens.

Chapter Thirty-Three

Courage to die

"Courage to die is the ultimate act of surrender;
It is a love affair with the unknown."

There once lived a dangerous man called Angulimala. Angulimala was the man who wore a garland of human fingers. He had taken an oath to kill one thousand people. He would take one finger from every person he killed, so that he could remember the count. He had made a garland of these collected fingers. He had collected nine hundred and ninety-nine fingers, only one more to go to complete his goal of thousand fingers.

He lived in the forest and awaited every day for someone to pass through that area. When someone did, he would kill them and add one finger of the victim into his garland. All the nearby villages knew this path was the most dangerous. One would be risking their life travelling in this path. No one took this road. As strangers to the place may not know about the danger that awaits, the king had appointed guards at the entrance of the road so that no one could take that road. This road remained closed.

Gautama Buddha, while passing through the area, entered that closed road. The guards stopped Buddha, and said, "This is not the road to be used. There is another path that will lead to your destination but this road is closed. This is the place where the dreaded Angulimala lives. Unless you are looking to sacrifice your life, do not go in this route."

It was known in the village that the only person who could have travelled this route was Angulimala's mother. The last time she visited him, he said to her, "Now only one finger is missing, and I spare you because you are my mother. But let this be a warning, if you ever come another time and I have not got my thousandth finger, I will not let you go back. I am waiting for that one finger desperately. Up to now I have not killed you because other people were available, but now nobody comes this way except you. So I want to warn you that next time if you come, you will be responsible for your visit, not me". Since then even she stopped visiting Angulimala.

The guards warned Buddha, "Do not take the risk." But Buddha said, "If I do not go then who else will go? There are only two things possible: either I will change him, or I will be his thousandth finger so that his desire is fulfilled." and continued, "I cannot miss the opportunity. I am anyway going to die one day. Sacrificing my head to Angulimala will be at least of some use. One day anyway I will die and you will have to burn my body. If I give him the thousandth finger, at the least I can fulfill his desire and give him peace of mind. Either he will have to kill me or I will kill him, but this encounter with Angulimala has to happen. You just lead me to him."

The guards said, this man is crazy, he wants to go into the mouth of death. Buddhas disciples who followed him became afraid listening to Buddha. The Guards said, "you are a crazy man it looks like and we are unable to convince you. We shall show you the direction, but you are on your own after that." Buddha said "Ok, that will be very kind of you". The disciples who always were eager to be as close to Buddha as possible, now started slowing down. As they walked the dreaded route, much gap started to build. Soon the disciples were miles away behind Gautam Buddha. They were continuing behind as they were curious to see what will happen, but they were not ready to be too close to Buddha. Who knows if Angulimala would kill them instead of the Buddha?

Angulimala as usual awaited for someone to pass by. He was sitting on his usual rock, watching the road. Buddha was closing in and far away a faint visual appeared to Angulimala. Angulimala could not believe his eyes. A very beautiful man in orange robes was gracefully walking towards him. He wondered, 'Who could this man be?', Angulimala had not heard of Gautam Buddha, but even this stone hearted Angulimala started feeling a certain softness towards the approaching man.

As Buddha came close, Angulimala holding a sharp sword in his hand, shouted, "Stop!". Gautam Buddha was just a few meters away, and Angulimala warned, "Don't take another step because if you do, I am going to take your life and the responsibility is not mine. You probably don't know who I am!"

> It is courage that puts the ego to rest, revealing the strength that lies in vulnerability and openness.

Buddha asked, "Do you know who you are?"

Angulimala was taken aback by Buddha's response. No one had questioned him back. Just looking at Angulimala would have terrified anyone and they would start to run. Angulimala said, "Your life is in danger! Neither is it the place nor the time to discuss such things."

Buddha said, "I think your life is in danger."

Angulimala laughed loudly and said, "I used to think I was the crazy one but you seem to be crazier than me. In spite of my warning, you are moving closer. You seem innocent, but don't think that my sword will spare you. I give you one last option, go back home now, otherwise it may be too late. I am just waiting for one more finger. I can find someone else, don't force me to take your life."

Buddha said, "You are blind. You are unable to see that I am not moving towards you but it is you who are moving towards me."

Angulimala said, "This is so very crazy! Anyone can see that you are the one moving. Look at me, I am standing without moving an inch."

Buddha said, "Nonsense! Since the day I came to know my Self, I have not moved a single inch. I am just centered, utterly centered with no movement. Look at your mind, it is continuously moving. You are asking me to stop but I have stopped very long ago. It is now time that you stop!"

Angulimala cannot believe Buddha is striking a conversation with him. Angulimala said, "You seem to be stubborn and impossible. You need a doctor to cure you. I have never seen such a mad man."

Buddha came very close, just a few feet away and Angulimala's hands for the first time trembled. The man was looking beautiful, harmless and innocent like a child. Angulimala had already fallen in love with Buddha. He had killed so many people but he had never come across a Buddha. He had never felt love. For the first time, Angulimala was feeling love. His heart was melting. There was a conflict between his head and heart.

Buddha said, "I am ready, but why is your hand trembling? You claimed you are a dreaded murderer, and even mighty kings are afraid of you. I am just a poor man with my begging bowl. I don't have anything. Go ahead and kill me, I will be immensely satisfied that I can fulfill your desire; my life has been useful, by your killing me, my death also would have been of some usefulness. But before you kill me, I just have one small wish, and I think you can grant me my dying wish."

Before death even the coldest and cruelest enemy is willing to fulfill any desire. Angulimala said, "It is a pity you are volunteering to die, tell me what do you want?"

Buddha said, "Look there, I want you to cut that branch which is full of flowers. I want to see those flowers closely, smell their fragrance and feel their beauty in this morning sun."

Angulimala with his sword cut the branch pointed by Buddha. Before he could give it to Buddha, Buddha said, "I hadn't completed expressing my last wish. This is only half the wish; the other half is, please put the branch back on the tree."

Angulimala said, "Since we spoke, I have come to realize that you are a crazy man. This must be the craziest death wish I have ever heard. How can I put this branch back on the tree?"

Buddha said, "If you do not have the power to create, you do not have any right to destroy. If you cannot give life, you don't have any right to give death to anything that is living."

There was silence in the forest. For the first time, Angulimala had lost his words. Angulimala's sword dropped on the ground. This silence was the moment of transformation. Angulimala fell down at the feet of Buddha, and said, "I don't know who you are, but whoever you are, you have awakened me with your words. Please take me as your disciple and initiate me."

By then the followers of Buddha had come closer. Seeing that Buddha was still standing and Angulimala at his feet, they mustered courage to come even closer. They remarked, "This man cannot be initiated, he is a murderer. And he is no ordinary murderer, he has murdered nine hundred and ninety-nine innocent people!"

Buddha said, "If I don't initiate him, who will initiate him? And I love Angulimala, He is a man of courage. I see a tremendous possibility in him. He has fought against the whole world. Without courage, one cannot stand against the whole world. Until now he was standing against the whole world with his sword; now he will stand with a consciousness which is far sharper than any sword. I had told you earlier that a murder was going to happen today. It was either me or Angulimala. Now, Angulimala is no more."

Buddha initiated Angulimala in this way.

Angulimala was no more the same, death had occurred. In that moment of silence, when he dropped his sword and fell to the feet of buddha, he was reborn a new man. Life happens, when one is courageous enough to surrender.

Chapter Thirty-Four

Impermanence

"Due to Impermanence,
There is always something new."

Only when one understands death, can one understand what is Life. This is the paradox of Life. This has been the quest of Siddhartha to know why disease? why old age? and why death?

Life is a continuous progression towards death – towards impermanence. If everything is progressing towards impermanence, then what is the whole purpose of life?

The word death is quite intimidating. It evokes feelings of loss and grief. The uncertainty of what happens after death can instill fear in us. Some develop anxiety hearing this word. It is important to have courage to introspect this word as it is the ultimate reality of life. It would have been nicer and more appealing if we say, Life is a continuous progression towards equilibrium. But, doing so would deprive you of knowing something about your Self – your fear of death. Observe the emotions, the thoughts that you experience when you hear the word death.

Death can also be defined as a state of equilibrium. Death means, there is no more life. It is over. The electrocardiogram shows a flat-line when the heart stops beating. Flatline and Equilibrium refer to a state of stability or lack of change. The line has no more ups and downs, is no more sinusoidal. Life has arrived at its state of equilibrium. We can say life is tending towards impermanence and culminates at a point of equilibrium. We call it death. On the contrary, life doesn't stop here. From this point on, life starts to disintegrate and takes newer forms. This is life continuum.

The origin and nature of the universe have been subjects of fascination and contemplation for humanity throughout history. The quest to understand the universe's creation and existence has led to various philosophical, religious, and scientific inquiries.

Entropy for example, uses the language of order and disorder. It is a concept borrowed from the laws of thermodynamics. It describes the inexorable tendency of systems to evolve from order to disorder. Entropy refers to a measure of disorder. It represents a fundamental principle in the physical sciences, indicating the universal progression from structured states to randomness. As time increases, the randomness also increases. When the randomness reaches its peak, a state of maximum entropy, it achieves a state of equilibrium.

In simple terms, Entropy is like a messiness level. Imagine a child has a box of colorful lego blocks, and they are all neatly stacked in a tower. That's low entropy when the toys are organized. But when a child starts to take the blocks out of the tower and scatter them around the room, that's high entropy. It is like when the toys are all over the place, it feels a bit chaotic. So, entropy refers to how messy or organized things are.

Entropy describes the inexorable tendency of systems to evolve from order to disorder.

All systems over time, move from low entropy to high entropy. Maximum entropy, is like the final stage when things have become as random or as disordered as they can get.

In the context of planets and cosmos, the universe is expanding, and galaxies are moving away from each other. As this happens, scientists predict that the entropy of the universe is increasing over time. 'Heat death' is a theoretical scenario where, as the universe continues to expand, everything gets more and more spread out. Eventually, stars burn out, galaxies drift apart, and the universe reaches a state of maximum entropy. In this state, there is no more energy available to do interesting things, like fuel the stars, or power life processes. The universe becomes highly uniform and essentially reaches a state of 'thermal equilibrium', where everything has the same temperature, and no interesting processes can take place. It is a state of rest, where no more change or action can occur.

Consider the hot cup of coffee. When you first pour it into a cup, it is hot, and the heat is concentrated. As it sits on the table, it cools down, and the heat starts spreading into the room. At some point, the coffee and the air around it will be the same temperature, and no more heat will flow. This is when you have reached equilibrium – the heat is evenly spread, and there is no more net flow of heat.

All life forms are tending towards disorder. This could help us understand why life gets complicated as time progresses. Think of your body as a town, and each cell in your body is like a tiny citizen. These cells are always busy doing their jobs, like building and repairing things, just like people in a town who are always working and keeping everything in order. In due time, the town of cells start to get disorganized. Imagine your cells as construction workers. To upkeep your body, they need energy. When your body is young and healthy, these workers are full of energy, and they can keep things in good shape. But as time goes on, your cells start to get weak. They lose efficiency and start to make mistakes. The town becomes a bit more disorganized – that is entropy at work. Over a period time, cells lose their energy, and they cannot do their jobs properly. The town becomes very, very messy, and everything stops working. When the cells get so disorganized and messy that it cannot do anything useful anymore, the cells reach a state of rest. The cells are now said to be dead.

The 'heat death' is like the point where your cells have lost so much energy that they cannot keep your body in good shape anymore. It is a bit like when a town falls into chaos because no one is working to maintain it.

The degree of randomness in our body has to be kept under check so that it does not reach the maximum state of randomness. This phenomenon of movement towards high degree of randomness is happening to all forms of life. To keep this in control, one needs energy and we consume food.

Imagine a plant, if it is not given the right nutrients or water, its progression towards it death increases rapidly. The plant starts to dry up and disease sets in. This indicates the high degree of randomness or high entropy. Even inanimate objects such as a car, if not maintained, gathers dust and parts start to disintegrate. All metal starts rusting. The car over a period of time will stop functioning. Entropy is not only a phenomena within the system, it is outside of a system too.

Life forms have designed themselves to consume energy and transform it such a way that they can regulate the state of randomness. Life forms consume food, and excrete that which is not useful. Note that this excretion also is increasing or adding to the entropy outside the life form. So, in this way, life forms influence the entropy of other life forms or the environment. There is entropy all around and we are in constant exchange of energy.

The psychological dimension is no different. The physical dimension affects our emotions and state of mind. Similarly, psychological states affect the state of physical. The mind is in constant movement, at times mind is racing, fueled by a wave of emotions leading to a state of chaos. Simply observe and be a witness to what is happening within you. We are all in the game of entropy.

Thoughts also have a lifecycle. Thoughts appear, and when you feed the thoughts, they grow and often multiply, thoughts transform in to other thoughts. When you do not feed thoughts, they disintegrate and thoughts are no more. In the context of entropy, you can think of ordered and structured thoughts as having low mental randomness. When you are focused, organized, and thinking clearly, your thoughts are in a state of low entropy. You have a clear, structured, and organized mind. On the other hand, thoughts can become chaotic and disordered, akin to high mental entropy. When your mind is scattered, and you are easily distracted, your thoughts are in a state of high entropy. It is like a mental 'mess' where you might struggle to concentrate or make decisions. Just as entropy is related to the amount of information in a physical system, in the realm of thoughts, you can associate low entropy with meaningful, useful information. High entropy, in this context, can be likened to mental noise, where irrelevant or conflicting thoughts create confusion. Such thoughts can be life destructive.

Memory also has entropy. If we continuously recall memory, the memory stays fresh. But if we do not recall, it fades away. Our physical entropy also affects memory, as time passes and we get old, we tend to forget details and experiences, leading to an increase in mental entropy. Memories fade, and thoughts become less organized.

Emotions also have entropy. They influence the entropy inside you (state of mind), and outside you (the resulting actions). Emotions grow increasingly intense and disordered if left unchecked, leading to emotional chaos.

For instance, unresolved anger can turn into rage, or sadness can spiral into depression.

The same analogy can be applied to all facets of life, organizations, businesses, commodities, institutions, societies, communities and personal relationships. Our life is shaping every moment through the forces that affect entropy. We may now come to appreciate the need for rules and discipline and their role in managing entropy in everyday life.

Within this entropic dance of the universe, there exists a delicate balance between order and chaos. Practice of Stillness can be seen as the door way to bring about this balance. A mental reset that brings order to the chaos of your mind.

Chapter Thirty-Five

Balance

यदा यदा हि धर्मस्य
ग्लानिर्भवति भारत ।
अभ्युत्थानमधर्मस्य
तदात्मानं सृजाम्यहम् ॥ ७ ॥

Yada yada hi dharmasya
Glanirbhavati bharata
Abhythanamadharmasya
Tadatmanam srijamyaham

TRANSLATION:

Whenever there is a decay in righteousness
and an increase in unrighteousness,
O Arjun (Bharata), at that time I manifest myself.

~Bhagavad Gita

The Upanishads are focused on the philosophical aspects of life, on spirituality and enlightenment. Maitri Upanishad explores the concept and nature of Self. It tries to answer the questions on joy and liberation. It has the first reference to the fundamental qualities called Gunas. The three Gunas – Rajas, Tamas and Sattva, influence the nature of all things in the universe, including human behavior and experience.

Rajas has the nature of movement. A quality that is energetic, that gives velocity. Tamas is the opposite. A quality that has the capacity to stop. It indicates inactivity, a state of inertia. Sattva is something that brings balance. Sattva is essential to balance the opposing qualities of Rajas and Tamas.

Imagine a triangle, the two vertices at the base are Rajas and Tamas. Sattva is above the two, the third vertex. The Triangle symbolism can be seen in many cultures.

The scientific minds of the Vedic period, have given the names – Rajas, Tamas and Sattva, for the three qualities of Nature. The ones who were poetic, metaphorical, they named them – Bramha, Rudra and Vishnu. They are representatives of the same three qualities. Brahma is the creator – Rajas; Rudra is the destroyer – Tamas; and Vishnu is the balancer, sustainer, representing – Sattva. For life to happen all three are necessary. Those who thought in terms of colors, identified them as Red, Black and White.

Modern scientific community recently discovered the atom. An atom comprises of proton, neutron and electron. Neutron do not contain any charge and are inactive. They represent Tamas. Electrons are negatively charged and are always in motion, they represent Rajas. The protons are positively charged, they are not in an agitated state, at the same time, they are not inactive either. They represent sattva.

Existence and all life forms, is a play of these qualities. What we experience as emotions, feelings and passion can also be mapped to the three Gunas. All qualities, positive and negative, that bring action: Passion, anger, fear, stress and anxiety are all said to be Rajas. They bring movement. Feelings such as sadness, grief, depression and laziness are that of Tamas. Qualities such as love and compassion are that of Sattva.

Life is a balancing act. Too much of anything is unhealthy. During the day you are active, at night you rest. If there is an imbalance in your activities or state of rest, then you are said to be unhealthy.

All the good and bad are in us. Nature of anger is that of fire. When anger brings Hell, the fire is hot. When it helps in one's development, the fire is cool. Anger can become a weapon of destruction or a tool for development. In competitive sports, if you can channel feelings of frustration with your performance to something positive, it can fuel your motivation to stay focused and improve. If one is too angry, it can be said that Rajas is not in balance.

> Once you sow the seed, the sun, the rain and soil start acting on the seed by providing nourishment for it to grow.

Similarly, in Tamas, there is both negative and positive. When you are sad, you become closed, movement stops. In sadness you are suffering. When you fall asleep, you are in a state of rest. In fact, Tamas is essential if you want to sleep. Role of Tamas is significant. Too much of sleep is also unhealthy. It can be said that Tamas is not in balance.

When you understand these forces and their influence on your being, you move towards a state of balance. Every emotion can be channeled to become creative and positive. Awareness is that which balances. In your awareness you rise above the dualities. This is Sattva. You strike a balance in your movement between two extremes.

When you ride a bicycle or motorcycle, tilting the vehicle to one side requires counterbalancing by adjusting your body position to stay upright. If you do no counterbalance, you will lose your stability and may fall. This is the nature of things. But let us suppose you fell down, and you look for why you met with this accident, who is responsible for this? is it bad luck? is something wrong with your fate? is there an evil force behind all this?

The problem, is always someone else, isn't it? And yes! there is someone responsible for why you fell down, what we call as gravity. While cycling you lost your balance and gravity did its job. So, blame it on gravity! Even when you walk, if you do not walk properly, you may fall. The reason the accident happened is just because you were not aligned with the nature of things. When you fall off a bicycle, don't look for who did it outwardly. When you are in a state of unawareness, you term such falling as accidents.

When you remain fixed on your seat and tilt the bicycle, you will fall, even if you don't want to. Similarly, when you are identified with your ego and emotions, you end up suffering, even if you did not intend to. Suffering simply follows. It is attracted towards your fixations, attachment and identifications to various aspects of life. This is nature playing its part. If you are loving and kind, happiness simply follows. The doer is you. When you are choosing to be angry, you are allowing suffering to happen. You cannot be in the grip of anger, without your permission to take control of you. As a result, you invite suffering.

What defines the extent of your suffering, or its absence, is the limit or threshold. When you ride a bicycle without limits, there comes a point where you lose control; no amount of braking will stop the bicycle, and braking may even throw you off balance. If you exceed the speed limit, an accident is bound to happen. Similarly, an emotion translates into thought, which further translates into words that are spoken. In anger, the words that you have spoken may have crossed that boundary, and you can no longer take back what you have said. There was a moment when it could have been under control, and you would not have spoken those words.

Introspect on how we react to life situations. It is possible to bring yourself to balance when you are within limits. If you go beyond limits, you lose control. Everyone is subject to stress. Where there is thought, there is stress. We cannot say 'do not get stressed'. An imposition of not to get stressed is also stress. What we mean is to avoid taking stress to the extreme point of breakdown. If the limit is crossed, one will eventually break down. This is the breaking point – the limit.

Freedom is not free; it comes with responsibility. When you understand the forces of nature and make yourself available to this wisdom, life becomes a playground. You experience freedom and liberation.

The nature of fire is to burn, it is hot. That is what is called the dharma of fire. Dharma means – the nature of things. Anger is fire manifested. You may feel angry and the result of it could break hell in your relationships. But once you come back to your senses and see that hell has broken, you may want to go back in time and fix it, but this may not be possible. You have allowed anger to cross the threshold.

Once you sow the seed, nature takes over, everything starts to act upon the seed whether you like it or not. The sun, the rain and soil start acting on the seed by providing nourishment for it to flourish. We can observe that existence is in movement towards the seed. The whole world conspires for the seed to sprout and grow in to a plant or tree. If you do not know about the seed, time will make you realize its potential. You come to know something of the seed. If you sow the seed of anger, then forces of existence starts acting over it. They work to bring the seed of anger to fruition, which results in suffering. This is anger manifesting. You sow the seed of love and kindness, all that is good start their movement towards you. This is the nature of things and the law of attraction. Existence wants to fulfill that which you are seeking. In your action you sow a seed, and you find that existence takes over to bring fruition to this seed. The seed you have sown is busy manifesting itself, and existence is merely an enabler.

We know that not all plants and trees yield flowers and fruit at the same time. Some yield early, while others may take a long time to bear fruit. Similarly, the consequences of anything good and bad may have a varying span. Existence does not stop until the seed sown is brought to fruition.

We often also find ourselves caught with with the conflicts of language and expression. We are all unique and so is our tendency to language, words and ideologies. If you perceive the three qualities of nature with a creative, imaginative mind then you may be able to align with or express nature in the terms of Bramha, Rudra and Vishnu; With a scientific mind, you express the same three qualities as Rajas, Tamas and Sattva; or you represent it as electron, nucleus and proton. For a painter or an artist, express it visually through colors such as white, black and red or geometric shapes, such as triangle etc. An artist can speak the language of beauty. A scientist cannot speak the same language. It is just not in his vocabulary. For a scientist, beauty lies in the scientific calculations and mathematical models. A song writer may describe the same truth through songs and praises of the divine. A mystic speaks a language of metaphors. Every master has expressed the same truth in their own unique ways. They are many rivers from the same mountain. It is necessary to recognize the water flowing in all the rivers is coming from the same source. These diverse perspectives add richness to our human existence. In the path of self-discovery, we are bound to confront the many faiths, teachings and practices. As we expand our openness in our practice of Stillness, we can realize the merging of all boundaries. One of the greatest experimenters in recent history is Paramahamsa Ramakrishna, who after his self-realization, did not stop his enquiry. He is known to have explored and actively practiced all the various faiths. He realized that all faiths are different paths leading to the same goal of realization, emphasizing the unity of faiths.

When Sri Krishna says, "*Whenever there is a decay in righteousness, and an increase in unrighteousness, at that time I manifest myself.*" He is referring to the aspect of bringing about balance. Krishna is saying awareness is the way to bring about balance. When he refers to himself in '*I manifest myself*', it is not about his ego – he is referring himself to awareness – supreme consciousness.

In awareness you see things as they are. You recognize that all the forces of creation and destruction are within you. They do not act all by themselves unless you allow them to take control of you. You are the doer, the decision maker, you are God and the Devil. You are the guardian of the gates to Heaven and Hell.

Chapter Thirty-Six

Aloneness

"Aloneness is an indicator of your spiritual readiness."

The mind is always seeking engagement, constantly looking for entertainment. It can be with anything. The moment the mind is not occupied, it gets restless. When you are alone, observe your behavior. You are unable to just sit quietly; you will feel the urge to do something – turn on the TV, change the channels, pick up your phone to call someone, check your social media, browse through emails, or read a newspaper. For no particular reason, you seek engagement. In this way, the mind relies on external distractions to feel at ease. It seems we are afraid to encounter ourselves when alone.

If the mind is all alone, it is not at ease, and due to this you may say "I am feeling lonely". When no one is around, you feel lonely, afraid, and also may feel depressed. But has it occurred to you that 'you' are simply uncomfortable being with yourself? This is not a good state to be in if you are not comfortable with your own Self. This feeling of loneliness arises from the habit of always indulging with something or someone. Your mind creates a sense of lack in your life, leading to fear and prompting you to try to compensate for these shortcomings.

> The purpose of Stillness is to transform you from your loneliness to aloneness.

This habit of constant indulgence with the external world is the reason why sitting in Stillness is a challenge. It is very difficult to sit, let alone practicing Stillness. Hence schooling, practice and discipline become important. You may experience struggle and discomfort sitting in Stillness. Your mind always keeps saying 'this is enough, you have sat for a long time'. Even if your sitting has not been more than ten minutes. This very attitude needs to bc witnessed. It is your mind that is looking for engagement. Your mind is telling you, that 'you are lonely', for its own gain.

The purpose of Stillness is to transform you from your loneliness to aloneness. Aloneness means you are comfortable with yourself. This happens when you are able to enjoy your own company and be joyful. Aloneness is a positive state of being. In loneliness, your mind is; in aloneness, there is no mind. The mind is silenced. You are no more dependent on your mind. With aloneness comes independence and freedom. You realize that you are complete and lack nothing.

Chapter Thirty-Seven

Butterfly

"No Freedom without responsibility"

When everything is going well, it is your doing. You want to take credit. When things are not going well, it is someone else's doing. You try to find out who is the person who is responsible for the situation you are in. 'There should be someone!'. This is the rationalization by the mind when one is unaware and unconscious in his actions.

Responsibility is your ability to respond. When you seek to identify who is responsible, it often indicates a loss of your capacity to respond.

From your very childhood, you have been depending on others – Parents, teachers, traditions, books, all kinds of dependencies. You have a support system. Someone has been there to take care of you. We are so used to being taken care of for years, that we are in a grip of inertia.

Learning to be responsible for oneself takes effort and does not come easily. There comes a time when you have to demonstrate accountability and become responsible for your actions. You have to stop depending on others and be self-reliant.

A great fear arises when you are on your own and must take responsibility. You may feel unprepared, as you have not put in the necessary hours of training. Responsibility can seem overwhelming, and your mind may play tricks on you. When things do not go your way, you might find yourself searching for someone to blame for your suffering.

In a state of unawareness, you go on reacting to the situation. In awareness – you respond. In responsibility, you own up to the situation, you take action. In unawareness, responsibility becomes a burden.

> In unawareness, there are choices. Awareness leaves you with no choice. Awareness is choiceless.

A student once caught a butterfly in his palms and went to the master. He asked the master "Can you tell if the butterfly in my palms, is alive or dead?", The master replied, "It is in your hands".

Life is a gift. The gift of life is in your hands. Whatever you make of your life is your own doing. In life it is okay to try, experiment, fail, explore, compete, win or lose. All these experiences add richness to your life. The true test of your understanding in life, is in your ability to respond to life situations, failures, and adversity. What choices do you have when things do not go your way? what are you going to do about it?

In unawareness, there are choices. Awareness leaves you with no choice. Awareness is choiceless. A man of understanding takes action. You simply do what needs to be done.

In awareness, you end the great divide. The mud has settled and the water is clear, and you bloom like a lotus flower silently in awareness.

FLOWERING

Chapter Thirty-Eight

Spaciousness

"The mind settles in silence;
The heart awakens in Stillness."

A Sufi mystic lived with his wife in a small hut in a wild forest. It was late in the evening. It had started to rain. His was the only hut in the forest and there were no houses for many kilometers. Both the husband and wife were making arrangements to go to bed. The small hut was just right for two people.

As they settled to sleep, they heard a knock on the door. The mystic said to his wife, "dear wife, please open the door. Someone may have got caught in the rain and may be looking for some help."

Knowing her husband, the wife gets angry and says, "There is no space for the two of us and you are asking me to accommodate another person?" The mystic said, "Look, this hut of ours is not a palace, two can sleep but three can sit."

The wife knew she could not win over this man, so she reluctantly went and opened the door. There stood a man drenched in rain. He said "dear madam, I am so sorry to have disturbed your sleep. I lost my way in this forest and I couldn't find another place to take shelter."

The forest was wild, he could not have gone any further. The Mystic from the inside replied, "You are welcome. Please make yourself comfortable. Our place as you can see is very small, two can sleep but three can sit" "I don't have much to offer you, but a few songs. We could hear from you about the world. We don't travel much and rarely do we get visitors." "Your visit has thrilled our hearts!"

The three of them sit close to one another and the mystic starts to sing a song. In the middle of the song, they hear another knock on the door.

This time the mystic asks the visitor to open the door. Three people sitting were already uncomfortable, looking at this situation, the visitor hesitated saying, "There is no space for any other person, we are not able to sit, how can we entertain any other person?" The mystic said, three can sit, and four can sit a little closer, a little more tightly, the weather is very cold and we could keep warm this way". Everyone sat very close to each other. The mystic's hut was packed. And the mystic continued his song.

A moment later, there is another knock. This was not a knock, it was more a kick on the door, and the mystic recognized the sound of the kick. It was that of the donkey that lived nearby. His wife was totally furious and the remaining two visitors also were angry and upset, that the mystic was planning to bring in the donkey.

The mystic said, "this is not a palace, four people can sit tightly, but five can stand, and it is not too long, the night is almost getting over and the dawn is approaching. That donkey needs our help" and "I shall sing a special song which all can enjoy".

So, the donkey was let in and he was made to stand in the center. All four of them stood around the donkey. The night passed. It was morning, and the mystic said to the parting visitors, "thank you for visiting, and I am sorry I could not offer you much".

> In Stillness, we discover the vast spaciousness within, where thoughts dissolve and peace and love expand.

This story is not a question of physical space, it is a question of spirit.

In the affairs of the world, the more you give, the less you will have. This is the economics of the world. If you distribute the money you possess, you will have that much less. But in the spiritual dimension, love is a reservoir that is ever flowing, the more you give, the more you have. When you have this spaciousness, you can uplift everyone around you.

It is a matter of scope. For example, a mother's scope is limited to her child. While a mystic's scope encompasses the whole world. Everyone is accommodated.

Only when you have something, you can share. If you have known real love, you can be loving. If you have not known love, what you probably think as love, is not love but an exchange for something. You are trading something in the name of love. Everyone is seeking or expressing love from the point of gaining.

For example, Parents might say, "I sacrificed everything for you," believing this reflects the depth of their love. But when love is accompanied by a sense of obligation or expectation, it is no longer unconditional. It becomes conditional affection, tied to repayment, directly or emotionally. From the child's point of view, what once felt like love now carries a hidden cost. What was given as "love" begins to feel like a burden, and the purity of the bond starts to erode. This is a form of psychological conditioning, where love, care, or sacrifice is taught to be repaid as duty, not something received freely. Over time, this creates emotional strain in families, partnerships, and even friendships. When love becomes a currency, it loses its essence. And when we pass on this conditioned model of love to others, especially to the next generation, we unknowingly perpetuate the cycle.

Raja, once fell over a bridge and was caught in the deep side of the river. His closest and best friend who happened to be with him rushed and pulled him out of the river and saved his life. Raja was grateful to him and expressed his gratitude. From that day on whenever Raja met his best friend, may it be on the street, in a family gathering, or over lunch, the best friend would remind him, "Do you recall, I saved you that day from the river". Raja was fed up of this claim. Every time he encountered his friend, the friend would say, "Do you recall, I was the one to save you from the river".

Raja decided to put an end to this. He called his best friend to meet him at the same place where he saved him. When they finally met, Raja jumped into the river and said, "Dear friend, please don't save me now. Go home". The friend was very puzzled. He did not understand the situation nor what Raja said.

Raja came out of the river all by himself, and his best friend never claimed that he saved Raja's life again.

If you have never experienced true friendship, then giving and sharing is merely a matter of convenience and gain. Similarly, what we call as true service is not really so, there is always some reason why we are at service. For example, when we are in service of the needy, we are doing it in the context of ourselves. When we feel the need to serve or help, it may be because we are uncomfortable seeing someone else suffer, and we are trying to satisfy our own feelings; otherwise, our mind is not at ease. It is questionable if there is true altruism. Something to be contemplated.

We are taught, '*The left hand should not know what has been shared by the right hand.*' True service is when you are no more and only the service remains. But this seems all too idealistic in today's world. This aspect of true love, true service is something to do with our spirit and our spaciousness. It does not fit within the context of worldly economics. The practice of Stillness enables this spaciousness within you. As you develop your Stillness, this spaciousness expands.

Chapter Thirty-Nine

Morality

"Morality cannot be practiced."

Ekido and Tanzan were walking down a muddy road. It was raining heavily and the road was very slippery. Just around the corner of an intersection, a beautiful girl was in her silk kimono was standing unable to cross the road. When Tanzan and Ekido reached the intersection, Tanzan said, "Come on, girl" and at once he lifted her in his arms and carried her over to the other side of the road. Ekido was a bit taken aback but remained silent until the night. He could not control anymore, he then asked, "We monks are not supposed to go near females, particularly not young and beautiful ones. Why did you do that?". Tanzan said, "I left the girl by the road long back, are you still carrying her?"

Morality has to be effortless. Morality cannot be acquired with practice and percepts. This is the paradox. Most teachings are prescriptive in teaching morality for one's spiritual attainment. The whole conditioning is that unless you get better in morality, you cannot be spiritual. In the beginning, conditioning of percepts may be necessary. Morality means to be truthful, to be compassionate, to be kind, not to commit adultery and so on. But how can morality be imposed? When I say imposed, I don't mean imposed from the outside, but our own moral policing that takes place within us. As you go deeper in your practice, you should also question all that is acquired. Self-discovery is about understanding our true nature and in doing so you will also need to confront your morality.

> When you are centered, morality arises naturally. There's no need to impose it.

Once you are centered in your Self, morality arises on its own. Morality is a side effect of your centeredness. One need not be fixated on morality. All you need to know is how to be centered. By being centered, you already know it. If you are fixated with morality, outwardly you may seem to be a moral person, but inside you remain immoral. Something is being suppressed due to the imposition of morality. The thoughts of what is immoral and what is moral will keep bothering you.

Ekido was an accomplished monk, but his mind was bothered by morality. He waited until the night to ask his concern to Tanzan. He had tried to repress his thoughts.

All day, he was constantly fighting his thoughts, whether to ask or not to ask. This is hypocrisy. His mind was invested in the immorality of things, always bothered about what is moral and what is immoral. He was not centered.

When you are centered, morality is very easy. You don't need to carry it anywhere. Here, Tanzan demonstrates such centeredness. Practice of Stillness is concerned with how you can be centered.

Chapter Forty

Forgiveness

"Stillness makes space for forgiveness."

Before you understand forgiveness, it becomes important to understand the word hate. Hate is an emotional response associated with intense feelings of deep dislike or hostility toward someone or something. Hate can stem from various reasons, such as past experiences, prejudices, misunderstandings, or differences in beliefs and values. Have you observed, those who are very close to you are the ones who hurt you the most. The closest friend has potential to become your greatest enemy. When you are filled with hate, it means you have taken a stance not to accept someone or a situation you are in. You simply resist accepting the circumstances that life has presented. This is your position, and hence you find yourself in a state of hate. This hate arises from your ego, which has decided not to accept life as it is. In doing so, your ego is invested in misery.

Experiencing sadness or anger is a natural reaction in moments of unawareness. However, if you continue to dwell in sadness, it can eventually turn into depression. Similarly, feeding anger over time can transform it into hate. These emotions consume your energy and leave you in a state where you feel powerless, trapped within their grip.

So how can you forgive?

It is not possible to forgive someone. It is just humanly impossible. The person whom you are angry with or whom you hate, cannot be forgiven. The very effort is futile. Forgiveness is not something you do only on the outside. The reason it is impossible because anger and hate are punishments that you have given to your Self.

If anger is fire, hate is fire with fury. A furious fire destroys anything that comes in its way. Much damage is caused to relationships when you are filled with hate. This is the nature of fire. It does not differentiate who will burn from its fury. Anything and anyone coming its way will be burnt. At the same time, it burns that which is fueling it. The fire of hate burns you from the inside, leaving scars for a lifetime.

The only person you can forgive is your Self. When you forgive your Self, you have forgiven your family, your friends, your parents and everyone else. When you forgive your Self, it means you have come to terms with your Self. You have accepted life as it is. You have accepted everyone as they are. In this deep acceptance of life as it is, the ego is no more. When you are in a state of acceptance, you accept everything – the good, the bad and the ugly. This is the nature of acceptance.

To accept your Self means to simply become available, in a state of let go. Let go does not mean not to do anything about your situation, but to become aware of your inner urge to be in control. When you are filled with hate, you are holding on to burning coal in your hands and not willing to let go.

Life does not wait for you, it keeps moving. In hate, the ego anchors itself in the past and hence you are unwilling to let go. Every moment, life is a possibility if you are available to it. Otherwise, all that remains is a state of misery. When you are not aligned with the movement of nature, you are not in balance. This imbalance causes misery. Life is always in the present. The past is your creation and future is your imagination. When you are attuned to life there is no past and there is no future. There is only this moment. Either you are available to this moment or you are not.

> The only person you can forgive is your Self. When you forgive your Self, you have accepted life.

When you are available to this moment, then life becomes a tremendous possibility. But if you are not available to this moment, then it simply means you are missing out on life. Misery becomes your only reality. When you become available to this moment, then you have accepted your Self. Doing so, you have accepted everything and everyone.

This is the practice of Stillness, to make ourselves become available to this very moment. Inhale….. Exhale…. follow the breath and watch the door swing. Embrace life in silence.

Chapter Forty-One

Compassion

"In Stillness we receive the world with compassion and clarity."

A certain master started committing petty crimes and would get arrested and go to jail. This happened many times. The neighbors who knew him were confused and worried. His students were not only getting upset by his behavior, they were also feeling ashamed as to how to call him their master.

The master would steal something small from his neighbors and then volunteer to admit that he committed the crime and would go to jail. Everyone knew him in the neighborhood. The master was a respected man. But now this was all changing as he had bothered all his neighbors. Even the police started to wonder why this man is doing what he is doing. Why is he going to jail to suffer?

As soon as he is let out of jail, he would go back to the neighborhood and steal something small again and go back to the police station to confess.

> The Journey of self-discovery culminates in Compassion, where love in its highest form simply overflows.

The neighbors and their students urged him to stop stealing. They said, if anything is required, they will bring it to him and there is no need to steal. But the master never listened. This happened for some time. One fine day, when the upset neighbors and students came to him, he said, "I know I have been very tough on you. I have bothered you much. Please forgive me for my actions." "I was stealing because this is the only way I could go to jail. There are many prisoners there. While you have many masters here who can help you. Who will help the prisoners?"

The master continued, "I could have gone in as a master, but the prisoners would not accept me or understand me. The prisoners understand the language of a thief. They get along with other thieves. In order for them to understand me, I had to be a thief. This is the reason I committed the theft."

The master in this way had been visiting the jail. In there, he transformed many prisoners.

Compassion is a quality where being kind, to care, to help are natural expressions. You are overflowing with love. Any overflowing emotion finds an expression. With this experience of overflowing love and joy, you are bound to express it through your kindness and compassion.

The Tibetan mantra 'Om mani padme hum', means 'supreme jewel is in the lotus'. Compassion is that jewel that you find in your awakening. Lotus symbolizes the awakening.

We all know the story of Jesus, the man who is a symbol of love. He is an embodiment of empathy, kindness and selfless love. During the crucifixion, Jesus exemplified profound compassion even amidst unimaginable suffering. As he hung on the cross, betrayed, beaten, and mocked, he prayed for his persecutors, saying, "Father, forgive them, for they know not what they do". His actions are a testament that true compassion transcends pain, extending grace and understanding even to those who cause harm.

As your practice in Stillness deepens, your realization opens your reservoir of compassion, where love, in its highest form, simply overflows.

Chapter Forty-Two

Gratitude

"In gratitude, your journey completes."

We often find ourselves complaining in life for many things. When we are focused on all the negatives, filled with complains, we are not sensitive to all the positives that life has bestowed upon us. Life has come to you as a gift. Everyone and all situations are enabling you to function in this world. Even adversity, bad situations, failures are all teaching you something and shaping you every moment.

The rice you eat has travelled a long distance from where a farmer first sowed the seed. Nature has done its job in nourishing the crops that transforms itself so that you can consume its produce. Parents have sacrificed their today, for your better tomorrow. Friends, colleagues and family have come together and given their love and support. Teachers have shared valuable knowledge, insights and wisdom only to make you better. Enemies have spent time and effort pointing your flaws and weakness; challenging you at every opportunity. They are the reason you have pushed yourself and become stronger.

> When you are filled with gratitude, it opens the possibility of knowing what real prayer is.

Your body is working round the clock to maintain itself. Pain and suffering have enabled you to know your inner strength. The sun, the earth, the air, the water and the fire, the space – all are sustaining you. Nature has bestowed you much love even in times when you never asked for it. When life is offering you so much, it is only human to be thankful. A thank you is generally directed towards someone and is an outward expression, but gratitude goes beyond a mere thank you. Gratitude is a deep inner feeling, an embodied experience, creating a deeper connection with oneself and the world. Invest your time to identify all that which is sustaining you. This will help you come out of the negative cycle of complaining towards life. When you enhance sensitivity to this whole existence and feel the connectedness to all that which is supporting you directly or indirectly, you will experience gratitude. Expand this sensitivity in your Stillness.

Ordinarily when we pray, we are kind of making a business deal with the gods of our faith to meet the many demands of our life. We also ask for the wellness of family, friends and the universe. There is nothing wrong with this. But it becomes important to differentiate such prayers. In such a prayer we are strengthening our Will. There is nothing wrong with it, but also understand that such a prayer is to do with the strengthening of ego. But when we are trying to understand ourselves, such prayer becomes irrelevant.

As your gratitude deepens, it transforms to reverence. When you are filled with gratitude, it opens the possibility of knowing what 'real' prayer is. When we are in deep gratitude, we surrender; we become the prayer. Surrender is not about surrendering to any person or any god in this context. Surrender is not an act of enslaving ourselves to someone. Such an act of surrendering to someone would mean that I am no more responsible for myself and there is someone else out there who will take all the responsibility. This is why we so freely take liberty to complain in life, because we don't feel responsible for ourselves. We make someone else, planets or our gods responsible. When you throw responsibility on someone else it is not surrender. Surrender is a conscious act of letting go of our ego in deep reverence to this Life. In doing so, you dissolve all boundaries and you become one with the universe. Prayer, then becomes a tool to dissolve the Self, where, only the prayer remains and you are no more. Such reverence to life expands your sense of connection to the world around you. It deepens your appreciation for all beings, fostering respect, empathy, and compassion. When you hold life in reverence, you begin to see the inherent value in every moment, every life form, and every experience, realizing that everything is part of a greater whole. Your gestalt changes and you begin to live more consciously giving a profound meaning to life. Life becomes a celebration. Reverence for life opens your heart and mind to the beauty and sacredness that exists in all things. This is also the fundamental essence of the path of Bhakthi or Devotion.

The path of Devotion and the path of meditation are oriented towards becoming one with universal self, but have a fundamental difference. This is something interesting to observe that in the path of meditation, the other is no more relevant and you begin with discarding all that is not you. You then dissolve yourself in to the ultimate state of no-self. This is what Buddha calls 'Anatta'. In the path of devotion, you are irrelevant and only the other is. Your effort is to dissolve into the other and become one with the other.

Gratitude, Prayer and Reverence are states of being where you no longer are present and only the experience remains, leaving only the pure awareness of the present.

Bowing is a ritual of expressing humility, gratitude, and respect. It is also used to express surrender to teachings or receiving blessings. When you experience gratitude, you do not need to observe this ritual, you bow naturally. Bowing becomes a happening and not your doing. Until you get to such a state, whenever you observe the ritual of bowing, bow mindfully and use this as a device and an opportunity for being mindful. When you bow, bow completely in all awareness.

Gratitude to life is possible when you have expressed gratitude to your own Self to start with. How often have you thanked your own body and mind? They are making the magic called 'Life' possible for you.

If you have not taken the moment, here is your moment. Close your eyes, take this moment to express your gratitude to your Self now. Stay in this feeling of gratitude for as long as you can.

Witness how your body and mind respond to your gratitude. Your whole being pulsates. This energy you experience within yourself is love. When you experience an overflowing of energy you may observe tears flow through your eyes naturally. When you have surrendered in gratitude you have found your reservoir of love and compassion.

In gratitude, your journey of self-discovery completes the full circle. You have arrived home.

ESSENCE

Chapter Forty-Three

Goose in a bottle

A baby goose (gosling) is raised in a large glass bottle. But the neck of the glass bottle was only enough for the gosling to be slid into the glass bottle. The neck of the bottle is quite small in circumference. The gosling was fed and well taken care of and it started to grow in the bottle. A day came when the gosling grew up to become a full-grown goose. The goose is so beautiful. But the neck of the glass bottle is so small that it seems like there is no way the goose can come out of the glass bottle. How is it possible to remove the goose from the bottle without harming the goose and without breaking the glass. Breaking the glass is not an option because if the glass breaks, the goose will be injured.

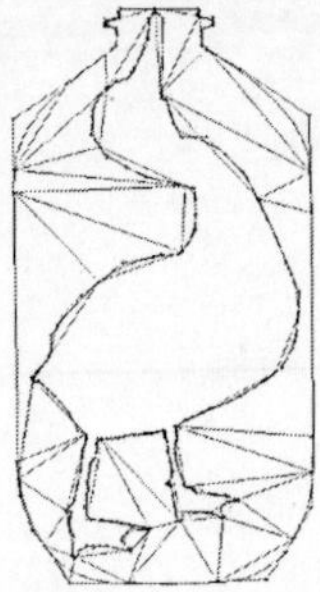

How can you get the goose out of the bottle?

ABOUT THE AUTHOR

Subhash Vasist embarked on the journey of self-discovery at an early age. He has spent decades investigating the science behind meditation practices and the psychology of human behavior. He is an explorer and adventure enthusiast. Subhash holds a Master's degree in psychology and is presently serving with a multinational firm. Subhash also teaches meditation in his free time and encourages individuals to embrace Stillness as a way to deepen self-awareness and foster personal growth. His straightforward and practical approach empowers individuals to cultivate a life of balance, clarity, and purpose.

Subhash is the author of "SILENSOPHY". The book offers readers practical wisdom and philosophical insights on Stillness and Self-discovery.

Insta/X **@subhashvasist**

subhashvasist@gmail.com

ACKNOWLEDGEMENTS

I would like to thank my family and friends for their love and support. To my wife, Nandini, for her unwavering patience and support.